You Can Touch the World

A How-to Manual for

Reaching the World for Christ

By Tom Shanklin

TSM Publishing
Mankato, Minnesota

Copyright

ISBN-13: 978-1461173908
ISBN-10: 1461173906

TSMPublishing
PO Box 4144
Mankato, MN 56002 USA
www.tomshanklin.org

I would like to dedicate this book to my three children, Heidi Hanzely, Nathan Shanklin, and Ruth Jackson, who have helped me to enjoy a taste of our heavenly Father's love for His children.

Contents

Foreword

Tom Shanklin is a bona fide 21st century evangelist. He lives and breathes with the passion to reach lost souls to come to know salvation in Christ. He understands his gift and calling to minister as an evangelist as one of the fivefold gift ministries found in Ephesians 4:11, "And he gave some, apostles; and some, prophets; and some, evangelists; and some, pastors and teachers."

Those who read this book will get a deeper sense of purpose on how and why we should reach the lost. Tom's personal experiences woven into each chapter bring life to each chapter to make for interesting reading. His chapter on "The Ministry of the Evangelist" is thought provoking to pastors who may not see the importance of the gifting of the evangelist in the Church today.

I commend this book by Tom Shanklin to your reading pleasure and for your own discovery as to the need for the voice of the evangelist in the Church.

Thank you, Tom, for your boldness in writing this book!

Pastor Virgil Amundson
Shell Lake Full Gospel Church
Shell Lake, Wisconsin

Acknowledgments

First, I would like to acknowledge the patient help, encouragement, and labor of love of my wife Susan in the writing of this book. Her tough critiques of my initial drafts forced me to dig deeper for the words to express what the Lord has put in my heart. Her partnership in life is a great blessing to me.

I also would like to acknowledge the following people, who among many others, helped to make this book a reality:

- To Pastor John Osteen, who planted the seeds for world evangelism in my heart many years ago. He has since gone to be with the Lord, but His legacy lives on in the heart and passion of many believers fulfilling their God-given assignments all around the world.

- To David Bergsland, who gave me hope that I could actually publish a book, and helped me to see it through.

- To Pastor Andrew Gackle, who has prayed for our ministry for many years and who read this manuscript and encouraged me greatly with this project.

- To Pastor Virgil Amundson, who inspired and encouraged me to touch the world by his example and his exuberant spirit.

- To my daughter, Heidi Hanzely, who used her editing skills to help fine-tune the language in this book and to my daughter Ruth Jackson for her valuable suggestions for the cover.

- To Carol Kaufman, who helped with proofreading and who has been an encourager to Susan and me for many years.

- To all the partners of Tom Shanklin Ministries, without whom we would not have been able to reach out and evangelize in order to learn by experience the principles that are communicated in this book.

Finally, I would like to give thanks to God for what He has done in my life and in the writing of this book. He has made me to progressively learn that the will of God is the most important thing. This is His project! It would not have been completed without the sincere conviction that He (the Boss) wanted it done. To God be the glory!

Preface

No matter who *you* are (*you* the pastor, *you* the dedicated mother, *you* the unappreciated department shoe sales person, *you* the Somalian goat herder), God has a plan for *you*! It's the plan you have been looking for to provide the total meaning and purpose of your life.

With Christ's direction and plan in your life, you *can* make a difference. You *can* have the power to bring change, to impart life that only comes from the heart of the Father. When you act on God's plan, you are acting out of love, out of concern, out of compassion. You are putting the throbbing heartbeat of the Father into action. His heart beats for people— lost, hurting, sighing, dying humanity—people who are far away from Him. You are the key to bringing them home. You are the extension of the heart of the Father.

Make contact. *Touch.* Extend your hand, your voice, your goods. Touching communicates "You matter to me!" Jesus touched people and they were changed. They were healed. They were freed. They left His presence different than when they came. You, too, are called to touch humanity, to inspire hope, and to bring change.

The world is the place you live and the people you see. It's the man at the Cenex gas station, the woman who cuts your hair, your insurance agent, your boss, even your spouse. *The world* is the nations and the isles of the sea. It's people of every tribe, nation, and language—people who need to feel the palpitations of the heart of Lord and the warmth of His embrace. You are uniquely created and commissioned by God to touch your world, and to leave it different than it was before.

This book was written for two reasons. One, it was written because of a burden for those who are away from God. And second, it was written because of an acute awareness that the way to reach those people is through other people. Not just the preachers, but everyone needs to get involved in this great mission. It's relational evangelism that will touch the world. That's what it's going to take to get people to God, everyone doing their part. It's a very simple plan for a confused world. This book is about your part in the plan. As you read, you will discover that you can make a difference, and that you can work together with others to see our Father's vision come to pass and to see His children come home.

I pray that something will be awakened in you—a divine quickening, an earthquake of compassion, a desire, a yearning born from heaven, and a confidence—and that you will truly comprehend that *You Can Touch the World.*

Tom Shanklin
Mankato, Minnesota, July, 2011

Chapter 1

The Heart of the Father

"And he said, A certain man had two sons: And the younger of them said to his father, Father, give me the portion of goods that falleth to me. And he divided unto them his living. And not many days after the younger son gathered all together, and took his journey into a far country, and there wasted his substance with riotous living." Luke 15:11-13, KJV.

I've known fathers whose children have gone away, children who never call, write, or come home for Christmas. It's a lonely pain. There's something missing. There's an ache within their hearts for completion, for fulfillment, for comfort, for family.

The Creator of the Universe is like that. He's yearning, waiting, and longing for His children to come home. It's His passion, His deepest desire, His ultimate mission. This is the message and purpose of the Bible. God wants us to know His great love for us. He wants to draw us to Himself and show us the way home.

For the Prodigal Son, life was all about "me, myself, and I." Tired of living under the confines of his father's house, he wanted to get out and see the world. He wanted to experience the "exciting" things of life.

I can relate to the Prodigal Son. My mother took me to church as a child, and when I was 9-years old, I responded to an altar call on an Easter Sunday morning at a Southern Baptist Church. Although I had a genuine experience with God that day, I did not fully surrender to the Lord. A few years later, I fell into a pattern of partying, alcohol use, and trying to please myself. I ended up far away from God.

Later as a college student in the '70s, I was drawn to the hippie culture, and my wife and I dropped out of college and traveled the United States in an old beat up pickup truck with a makeshift camper built onto the back. We were looking for peace and true happiness in remote areas with other free-spirited young people. While searching everywhere for peace, I kept coming up empty, lost, and confused.

Finally in 1977, I met a group of Christians who had been part of the long-haired hippie counterculture, but had come to faith in Christ. Through their influence and a dramatic personal encounter with the living God, I totally surrendered my life to the Lord. Like the Prodigal Son, I returned to my Father and experienced the joy that can only come by living in His house.

But the story of the Prodigal Son is a message for all of humanity. Our heavenly Father has begotten the human race. We were created as the offspring of God, made in His image. But, like the Prodigal, we have been in a far country, wasting our substance with riotous living. For him, it was a life of partying and spending, but there are other ways to waste your life, and there are other places far away from the Father—in a boardroom, a sports arena, a palatial home in the suburbs, in a Hindu temple worshipping a multitude of "gods," in the city or the country—so many children, so far away from home.

While the Prodigal Son was away, the father agonized. Each day he looked down the road in hope and anticipation. "Maybe this will be the day my son will come home." He cried hot tears, his heart breaking. While his son partied, the father suffered. He longed to embrace his lost son once again. He had let him go, not holding him by rule and constraint, even releasing to the Prodigal his inheritance, which he squandered on the pleasures of the flesh, wasting himself with his own self-centered pursuits. But the father waited.

When all of his resources were gone, the Bible says that the Prodigal "came to himself." He was empty and alone and in need of his father's love and care. The pursuit of pleasure had run its course and the love of the father drew him back home.

The Prodigal turned his eyes back toward his home. He repented, turning away from his own stupidity, resolving in his heart to return home. He saw the emptiness of his pursuit and remembered the love of his father. He said, "I will arise and go to my father, and will say unto him, 'Father, I have sinned against heaven, and before thee, And am no

3

more worthy to be called thy son: make me as one of thy hired servants.'" Luke 15:18, 19, KJV.

Not only did the father long for the son, but down deep inside, the son longed for his father. This is the position of people all around the world. Internally they are "missing something." Down deep inside, there is a longing in their heart for that which was lost when Adam and Eve sinned in the Garden. As the Scripture says, "Wherefore, as by one man sin entered into the world, and death by sin; and so death passed upon all men, for that all have sinned:" Romans 5:12, KJV. When Adam fell, we all fell and lost our place of fellowship with the Creator God. We lost our connection to His love and resources. We were without God and without hope in this world. We were created for that fellowship, and nothing will be exactly right until we once again come home.

As the Prodigal returned, we envision him walking on the road, broken, no bounce in his step now, no boisterous boyish pride, just a heavy-hearted, battered, dispirited young man in need of a bath, a warm bed, and the comforts of home. Smelling like the pig pen where he had last been, he trudged down the road, wondering what sort of welcome he would find. After all, he had turned his back on those who loved him and had wasted the family fortune on prostitutes. Would his father even look at him, much less hear his plea for pardon?

The father was waiting, looking out the window as he did each day, studying the long winding road that led to his house. There he saw a figure of a man slowly making his way along the path. "Could it be? Could it be my son?" The profile looked like an old man. His shoulders were drooped. His head was down. His walk was listless, but instinctively the father knew it was his son coming home.

The father burst out the door and ran down the road. Crying out to a servant, he said, "Bring a pair of shoes, a ring, and bring the best robe. My son has come home!" He ran with all his might, the dust flying, his robe trailing, his heart beating, with labored breathing, stretching out with each step to once again see, "My son! My son!"

The Prodigal Son looked up in his despairing state to see this incongruous scene—father running for all he was worth, panting, to once again see his precious progeny, not waiting for him to enter the borders of the estate, not looking for an explanation, not demanding a groveling entreaty. No, rather he ran out to hug and kiss his son and to show a father's compassion for a lost, wayward, misguided son.

"And the son said unto him, Father, I have sinned against heaven, and in thy sight, and am no more worthy to be called thy son. But the father said to his servants, Bring forth the best robe, and put it on him; and put a ring on his hand, and shoes on his feet: And bring hither the fatted calf, and kill it; and let us eat, and be merry: For this my son was dead, and is alive again; he was lost, and is found. And they began to be merry." Luke 15:21-24, KJV.

My Son Was Dead

The person who is away from God is in such a state—empty, lost, and spiritually dead. As the Scripture says, "And you *hath he quickened*, who were dead in trespasses and sins;" Ephesians 2:1, KJV. Outside of Christ, every human being on the face of the earth is spiritually dead. He or she may walk, talk, make money, and produce tremendous intellectual arguments. He may seem to be spiritually enlightened. He may do charitable deeds, create profitable businesses, and perform astounding feats, but he is spiritually dead. He has no spiritual life. His separation from the Creator has severed his tie to the eternal, to the life of God.

Outside of Christ, he is without hope and without God. "That at that time ye were without Christ, being aliens from the commonwealth of Israel, and strangers from the covenants of promise, having no hope, and without God in the world:" Ephesians 2:12, KJV. We may think, "He is such a wonderful person. He's done good things. He dresses nice and talks nice. He must be pleasing to God." But if he is outside of Christ, he is lost. He is dead. He is an enemy of God. He is without hope and without God in this world.

But the Father is waiting. Ever since the Garden of Eden, we have been estranged, our hearts separated from the Creator. Like the Prodigal Son, we have been away from home. But our Father gave us a way back to Himself. He gave His Son to die for our sins, and once again to give us access to the Father's house. Father is "not willing that any should perish, but that all should come to repentance." 2 Peter 3:9, KJV.

The father was ecstatic about his son's return! "This my son was dead, and is alive again, he was lost and is found. My son has come home." (author's paraphrase) It was time to celebrate. Heaven rejoices over one sinner coming home, because it means one life which had been destroyed is now saved. One person who was lost has been found. "I say unto you, that likewise joy shall be in heaven over one sinner that repenteth, more than over ninety and nine just persons, which need no repentance." Luke 15:7, KJV. The heart of the heavenly Father today is for His children to come back to Him. The heart of the Father longs for His children to be restored, healed, made whole and free. Our Father gives good gifts to His children. The father brought out the best robe, which represents a robe of righteousness. It is a gift of acceptance, forgiveness, and royalty for those in God's family. Never mind that the son was most recently in the pig pen. All is forgiven now. The son is home. He is accepted and loved.

He brought out shoes for his son's feet. The shoes represent an ability to walk with God. We are not only forgiven, but also delivered from the power of sin through the cross of Calvary. The Holy Spirit writes God's laws in our hearts so that we might know and do the will of God. This likewise is a gift from our loving Father.

He put a ring on his son's finger. In biblical times men wore a signet ring with the family emblem. It could be used to seal an agreement. This would be like the Father giving check-signing privileges to his son. The son who had wasted the family fortune was now given authority to write checks on the family account. As God's children, we have been given authority in the name of Jesus to ask what we will and it shall be done. We can cast out devils and do mighty works through that name.

The father then killed the fatted calf and celebrated his son's return. When His children come home, our heavenly Father celebrates. He wants to give us His best and lavish His love on us. This is the heart of the Father.

Jesus said, "In my Father's house are many mansions: if *it were* not *so*, I would have told you. I go to prepare a place for you. And if I go and prepare a place for you, I will come again, and receive you unto myself; that where I am, *there* ye may be also." John 14:2, 3, KJV. Jesus died on the cross of Calvary to make a way for us to live forever in the Father's house. There is no other way to get to heaven but through the one true Savior, Jesus Christ. As He said, "…I am the way, the truth, and the life: no man cometh unto the Father, but by me." John 14:6, KJV

The Elder Brother Syndrome

When the Prodigal's older brother heard the music and dancing, he asked what was going on

8

at the father's house. "What's all the hoopla?" he may have asked. When he learned that his younger brother had returned and that father was throwing a party, he was angry and refused to come in the house. His father went out to encourage him to join the festivities. "And he answering said to his father, Lo, these many years do I serve thee, neither transgressed I at any time thy commandment: and yet thou never gavest me a kid, that I might make merry with my friends: But as soon as this thy son was come, which hath devoured thy living with harlots, thou hast killed for him the fatted calf." Luke 15:29, 30, KJV.

The elder brother was like many Christians today, doing their religious duties by attending church every week, serving on committees, living in the culture of their church, trudging through the dry externals of religion, but not comprehending the love of the Father. Like the elder brother, many are serving, but have no zeal for what's important to the Father. They make no allowances for those who have gone away from Him. Some are more interested in getting credit for what they have done than in seeing lost and dying people restored to the Lord. They are in the Father's house but are sadly missing the point.

In His love, the Father brings a word of correction to those with the elder brother syndrome: "And he said unto him, Son, thou art ever with me, and all that I have is thine. It was meet that we should make merry, and be glad: for this thy brother was dead, and is alive again; and was lost, and is found." Luke 15:31, 32, KJV.

He was saying, "Son, you have everything you want or will ever need. You have me and all that I have is yours. You can have the fatted calf any day of the week. You should start living like a son, rather than a servant. Start enjoying your life with me. But just realize that my heart is for my lost son also. Now he has come home, and it's time for us to rejoice."

All around the world there are multiplied millions of Prodigals who need the Good News of the Father's love, mercy, and forgiveness. Our Father yearns for them to come home. He is looking out the window daily and watching so He can run out to meet them. May we draw close to Father and listen to His heartbeat for the lost. May we turn from selfish, introspective, unthinking, uncaring religion and give ourselves to our real purpose in life, bringing the Father's children home to Him.

Dear Father, give me Your heart for the Prodigals and for those that are away from home. Give me a heart that says, "I must tell them the Good News. I must tell them about the Father's love and His mercy. I must let them know that the way is made for them through your Son to come home and receive all your blessings." Give me that heart, Father, as I give myself to You, in Jesus' name, I pray. Amen.

Chapter 2

The Family Business

I must be about my Father's business?"
Luke 2:49, KJV.

When I was sixteen, I had a summer job stocking shelves and sweeping floors for a furniture store owned by a Jewish family. Fredman's Furniture Store sold furniture and a little bit of everything else in a rough neighborhood in St. Louis. I rode to work everyday with a man from my town who worked for the store as an accountant. Like me, he was an employee. At the store, there were employees, and then there were the family members.

As a teenager, my greatest interest was to get through the day, get my paycheck at the end of the week, and go out with my friends on Friday night. I plodded through my days, putting in my time and trying to keep my bosses happy. I really didn't care about "the family business."

The members of the family, however, were different. Whether serving as managers or cleaning the bathrooms, the family members had a bounce in their step and an enthusiasm for their work. They were focused, on track, and didn't watch the time clock. They were zealous and devoted to the family business.

For the Christian, the greatest revelation that we can receive is that we have been adopted into the family of God because of what Jesus has done for us on the cross and that the Creator of the universe is our heavenly Father. "And because ye are sons, God hath sent forth the Spirit of his Son into your hearts, crying, Abba, Father. Wherefore thou art no more a servant, but a son; and if a son, then an heir of God through Christ." Galatians 4:6, 7, KJV.

In fact, the Bible tells us that as children, we are heirs of God and joint heirs with Jesus Christ. Everything which belongs to Jesus belongs to us. So like those Jewish family members in St. Louis, we have a share in the family business, and throughout eternity we will enjoy the rewards of our labors here on earth.

For that business in St. Louis, the goal was financial profit. For us, however, the goal is souls. The Great Commission is to take the Gospel of the Son to the world and to let people know that "For God so loved the world, that he gave his only begotten Son, that whosoever believeth in him should not perish, but have everlasting life." John 3:16, KJV.

The Father did His part. He sent the Son. Jesus did His part. He died on the cross of Calvary for the sins of the whole world. We now are to do our part. "Go ye into all the world and preach the Gospel..." (Mark 16:15)

Every person in Christ's Body, the Church, has a part in God's family business. Like that store in St. Louis where I worked as a young man, there are many different jobs in the family business, but every job contributes to the harvest of souls. Some family members are evangelists to reach the lost and train the Body in evangelism. Some are church planters. Some are pastors to care for the sheep that come into the church. Others are in a supportive role. But all of us are called to be busy in the family business by reaching out to the lost, the hurting, and the dying of this world.

Every job is important. Whether we are serving as an usher, greeter, Sunday School teacher, guitar player, sound booth technician, missionary, pastor, homemaker, evangelist, or Christian businessperson, each of us contribute to the success of our Father's business. Each of us can count it our great joy and privilege to serve wherever God places us.

As God gives us opportunity, we must serve faithfully and humbly in order to progressively move into our particular role. We need to prepare ourselves to serve effectively. We should not take our position in the family business lightly. We should seek the training and develop the discipline necessary to effectively fulfill our particular ministry role. We should make it a lifetime practice to study and obey the Word of God, to pray and seek the Father's will, and to live a life filled with the Spirit. We all need to be ready to share the hope of salvation that is within us, and we should be diligent to live a life before others that reflects the glory of God.

In the furniture store where I worked, the family members were often given positions of responsibility and management, but first they needed to prove themselves in simpler tasks. Likewise, there is a time of development and growth for those who are called into leadership roles in the Body of Christ. Leaders must learn to become servants and learn to be faithful in small, simple tasks.

As you are faithful in little things, God develops strength and character in you, so that you might be strong for the assignments He has for you later in life. Use your time of development wisely. It's crucial to your success. No matter what job God gives you to do, always retain your sense of humility and a comprehension of the importance of your part in the mission. Make it your quest to discover that purpose and to move into a position of fruitfulness in the family business.

From an early age, Jesus had a great sense of purpose. He never digressed nor lost interest in the great cause of His life. Even as a 12-year-old boy, Jesus recognized His mission in life. He was deeply interested in what was dear to His Father's heart, which was to reach people for His Father. "For the Son of man is come to seek and to save that which was lost." Luke 19:10, KJV.

Many times, Jesus could have become discouraged and quit. The Scriptures tell us that He was a man of sorrows and acquainted with grief. He faced tremendous opposition and difficulties, yet He remained steadfast and focused, ever moving forward to fulfill His mission. He lived to please His Father, saying "And he that sent me is with me: the Father hath not left me alone; for I do always those things that please him." John 8:29, KJV. Jesus made a lifetime commitment to His Father's business.

Like Jesus, let us remain steadfast, faithful, and continually enthused, fulfilling the heart of the Father by bringing many children home to Him. It's time to be about the Father's business.

Dear Father, thank You for calling me and making me Your child. I'm glad to have a part in Your business, reaching this world with the Gospel of Your Son. Train me, Father, in the family business. Show me the special abilities that You have put within me to reach people for You and I will be careful to give You all the glory for what is done through my life, in Jesus' name. Amen.

Chapter 3

God Uses Ordinary People

"Now as he walked by the sea of Galilee, he saw Simon and Andrew his brother casting a net into the sea: for they were fishers. And Jesus said unto them, Come ye after me, and I will make you to become fishers of men. And straightway they forsook their nets, and followed him. And when he had gone a little further thence, he saw James the son of Zebedee, and John his brother, who also were in the ship mending their nets. And straightway he called them: and they left their father Zebedee in the ship with the hired servants, and went after him." Mark 1:16-20, KJV.

A preacher was once introduced to a lady. When he asked her what she did in life, she answered, "I am a disciple and a witness for Jesus Christ cleverly disguised as a factory worker."

Jesus calls us to become fishers of men. We are here to win the lost and make disciples. Each of us has a little different part to play in God's fishing operation, but understand, we all are essential to the plans and purposes of God. Some may be called as evangelists to great crowds around the world. Others may be working as missionaries in third world countries. Some are pastors and teachers who care for the the people that come into the church. Still others may be moms or dads, brothers or sisters, living normal lives amongst the people in their community as witnesses for Christ.

One day, the wife of a dairy farmer in Charlotte, North Carolina was giving her little boy a bath in a galvanized tub in the kitchen and taught him a Bible verse. She planted a powerful seed in her son's life that day. The little boy in the bathtub was Billy Graham, who still remembers the day his mother gave him a bath and quoted John 3:16.

The following account of the story was taken from a transcript of a Crusade in Brisbane, Australia, May 29, 1959. (The person, Leighton Ford, that he refers to in recounting the story is his brother-in-law and was an associate evangelist at the time.) Mr. Graham said: "Now Leighton Ford's mother-in-law is my mother. And when Leighton Ford's mother-in-law had me in a bathtub at the age of six in one of the old galvanized tubs—we lived way back on a farm. I'm just a farm boy. We lived way back on the farm, and she was scrubbing my ears. We took a bath every Saturday night. Now I don't understand why you laugh. Don't you take them that often? We took a bath every Saturday night, and my mother was scrubbing my ears. And she said, 'Son, I'm going to teach you something from the Bible.' And she taught me those twenty-five words. 'For God so loved the world, that he gave his only begotten Son, that whosoever believeth in him should not perish, but have everlasting life.'"(Courtesy Billy Graham Evangelistic Assoication)

Another ordinary person, a pastor from rural England in the 18th century began to be burdened in his heart for the people of the world who were dying and going out into eternity without Christ. He researched the nations of the world and the people, particularly focusing on their religions and spirituality. As he studied and prayed, his burden grew stronger. He later wrote a book called "An Inquiry Into The Obligations Of Christians To Use Means For The Conversion Of The Heathens."

On May 31, 1792, he preached a sermon to his fellow ministers at Nottingham, England. His vision was for the evangelization of the world. In that message, he dramatically proved the criminality of allowing the unsaved of this world to go to their grave and into a Christ-less eternity without hearing the Gospel of Jesus Christ. He said that the Church must immediately take action to promote the Gospel among the heathen masses of the world.

Although the sermon had a powerful effect on the listeners, no one had the courage or faith to act upon the challenge contained in the message. As the meeting was about to break up, he turned to his friend and fellow-minister, Andrew Fuller, and cried out with great emotion, "Is there nothing again going to be done, sir?"

Fuller was stirred in his heart and pressed the ministers to pass a resolution to form the "Baptist Society for Propagating the Gospel among the Heathens." Four months later 12 men committed themselves as the first members of the society. They contributed 13 British pounds to the cause which was collected in a snuff box. Thus began the missionary movement that is touching the world today. That rural pastor's name is William Carey. That ordinary pastor is considered to be the father of the modern missionary movement.

When William Carey gave his sermon in Nottingham, England in 1792, only 7 out of every 1000 Christians in the world were from the continents of Africa or Asia. By 1992, just 200 years later, the spiritual demographics of the world had been revolutionized as a result of the movement he started. By then, 580 of every 1000 Christians were from those two continents.

One person can change the world! As a result of this movement which began in northwestern Europe, millions have come into the Kingdom of God throughout the earth. Christianity, which in the eighteenth century was largely a western religion, has spread throughout the globe. This is an example of what can be accomplished by one person who is in earnest about the cause of Christ, especially if that one person can convince others to align themselves to God in the cause of evangelizing the world. (Source: "The Church is Bigger than You Think, The Unfinished Work of World Evangelisation," Patrick Johnstone, Christian Focus Publications)

You see, someone has to lead and someone has to follow and no one needs to be concerned about who gets the credit. Then, we can operate in the power of agreement and see great results for the Lord in this earth.

What can you do? It's not a matter of becoming great and famous. It's not about becoming Super Christian. It is just a matter of being faithful to God in the things He has called you to do.

Jesus didn't call people of great prominence in society or in education or in oratory skill. He called fishermen and hardworking ordinary people to follow Him. Sometimes we think that if God could just get a hold of a wealthy businessman or a great athlete or a singer, the whole world would change and everyone would want to come to Jesus. But God is not looking for people of influence so that He can drop their name in a conversation to impress someone. No! God is looking for people from every arena of life (rich and poor, famous and not so famous) who will humble themselves and allow His glory to be seen upon their lives. That is how He works.

Think of David the shepherd boy. The prophet Samuel, by the direction of the Holy Spirit, came to Bethlehem to anoint one of Jesse's sons as king over Israel. So Jesse brought out all of the strapping young men in his household to see the prophet. "And it came to pass, when they were come, that he looked on Eliab, and said, Surely the LORD'S anointed *is* before him. But the LORD said unto Samuel, Look not on his countenance, or on the height of his stature; because I have refused him: for *the LORD seeth* not as man seeth; for man looketh on the outward appearance, but the LORD looketh on the heart." 1 Samuel 16:6, 7, KJV.

Eliab looked good to the natural eyes, but God looked much deeper. Jesse proceeded to bring out six more sons, and each time Samuel said, "Neither hath the Lord chosen this." Then the prophet asked Samuel if these were all of his sons. Jesse said that he had one more, the youngest, who was out taking care of the sheep. When David was brought in, the Lord said to Samuel, "Arise, anoint him, for this is he."

"Then Samuel took the horn of oil, and anointed him in the midst of his brethren: and the Spirit of the LORD came upon David from that day forward. So Samuel rose up, and went to Ramah." 1 Samuel 16:13, KJV. So God took the shepherd boy, anointed him, and made him King over Israel. He takes the foolish things to confound the wise and the weak things to confound the mighty. Think of the many others that were small in the eyes of the world who God used to do great and mighty things. There was Abraham, a goat herder, Moses, a stutterer and a murderer, Mary, a peasant girl, and Esther, Gideon, and Deborah. All these were unlikely choices to become world-changers.

In the same way, Jesus took a group of rag tag fishermen, tax collectors, and political zealots to be the leaders of a movement to change the world. And

He will use you. You just have to be willing to follow Him wholeheartedly and allow Him to shape and mold you. Your part is to follow Jesus. His part is to make you a fisher of men. If you will be faithful in your relationship with Him and trust in His Word to you, He will bring the necessary changes to bring you into a place of fruitfulness in the harvest.

Following Jesus means consecrating your life 100 percent to the Lord. It means being willing to suffer for Him. It means denying your own selfish desires and putting His will first place in your life. Jesus said, "If any *man* will come after me, let him deny himself, and take up his cross, and follow me." Matthew 16:24, KJV. These are the people that Jesus uses to change the world, those who are sold out to Him. The world will not be won by a compromising Church, but a Church that is wholly following the will of God.

Jesus is calling us to forsake all and follow Him. He's calling us to leave our nets (the things of the world) and take up our cross and follow Him. This doesn't necessarily mean leaving your occupation, but it does mean putting God and His Kingdom first in your life. It means taking up Kingdom priorities and Kingdom purposes. When you do this, His promise to you is "I will make you fishers of men." Our job is to follow Him. His job is to "make us..." We provide the willingness. He provides the transforming power. He makes us fishers of men. We don't make ourselves. We don't have what it takes. But Jesus is more than up for the task. "For it is God

23

which worketh in you both to will and to do of *his* good pleasure." Philippians 2:13, KJV.

It is a total consecration of your life that enables Jesus to do His work. That day as He walked by the shores of Galilee, He called those fisherman to follow Him. They left their nets to follow Jesus. Imagine that. They left their families. They left their livelihood. They left their way of life to follow an itinerant preacher named Jesus. That must have been an incredible compelling force that drew these men. That force is the love of God! If you're a believer in Christ, then that force is in you also, and His love through you will draw people to follow Jesus.

Dear Father, I believe You can use me as a fisher of men, to rescue souls. I choose to deny myself, take up my cross and follow Jesus. Lord, make me a fisher of men. Help me to catch many people for You, in Jesus name. Amen.

Chapter 4

Align Yourself with Me

"But when he saw the multitudes, he was moved with compassion on them, because they fainted, and were scattered abroad, as sheep having no shepherd. Then saith he unto his disciples, The harvest truly is plenteous, but the labourers are few; Pray ye therefore the Lord of the harvest, that he will send forth labourers into his harvest." *Matthew 9:36-38, KJV.*

When God began to deal with me about the ministry of evangelism, these words began to come up in my spirit over and over again, "Align yourself with Me!" As I began to pray and seek Him, I realized that there was a misalignment between what was in my heart and in the heart of the Lord. I did not share in His level of passion for reaching the lost. My heart needed an attitude adjustment. This kind of change can only come through yielding to God in prayer.

If we are ever going to accomplish God's will in reaching a lost humanity, then we are going to have to experience a deep fundamental change. If we continue to follow our natural inclinations, then nothing of significance will ever take place. We may develop evangelism programs in our church and support missions, but the need is much deeper. Our heart must be changed so that God's heartbeat for a lost world will pound in our chest.

We must be supernaturally birthed into His purpose and into His vision. We need to get the heart of God, which only comes through prayer and intimacy with Him. We need to lean on His breast and hear His heartbeat. It beats for a lost, dying, crying, sighing humanity. His heart beats for the world!

When we see problems in those around us— where we work, in our community or even in our own family, our first response is to pray that the people around us will change. But what needs to happen first is that *we* must change. We need to have the Lord's compassion birthed in our hearts. We need to pray out of a spirit of love. We need to have a lifestyle that is aligned with the Lord, so that the people around us can see Jesus in us. Too often, we have presented religion to people instead of relationship and a form of godliness instead of the real power of God. We need to spend time with God in prayer and let Him anoint us for service. Then the people around us will see a true refection of Jesus and find the reality of the living Christ.

I'll never forget how prayer brought a major change in my heart during a missionary outreach in Kenya, East Africa. I was ministering the Word of God in an open air evangelistic crusade and a pastor's seminar. There was great hunger in the people, but my ministry was rather mechanical. My heart wasn't in it. I was fretting about problems in a church I was pastoring. I was lonely for my wife.

I just couldn't seem to be able to get into the flow of ministry.

One afternoon I had some rare time alone in my hotel room and I cried out to the Lord, saying, "This is ridiculous. These people have great needs and I'm here to minister to them, not to feel sorry for myself." I prayed, "Lord, give me Your heart for these people!" A transformation took place in that hotel room in a mountainous region of Kenya. I made a decisive faith connection with God on this issue. From that moment, the entire trip turned around. The connection I made with the Lord translated into a connection with the people, and there was much fruit from our labors. Many people came to the Lord in those meetings and many pastors from various denominations were greatly encouraged. We even heard a report of someone receiving Christ who was not in attendance at the crusade, but had heard the Gospel preached through the PA system.

As Jesus ministered to the people, He saw the great needs. They were scattered like sheep without a shepherd. Things have not changed all that much in 2,000 years. Today, the multitudes also are scattered. They are scattered about by all the philosophies of this world. They are scattered about by every demon-inspired religion. They are scattered by sensuality and greed. Many are scattered about by their own needs and problems, such as poverty, sickness, and emotional bankruptcy.

When Jesus saw the great spiritual famine around Him, He realized that He alone could not touch all the people. Help was needed. Laborers, Gospel workers were needed to take the message of the Kingdom to the people and to heal them. His first response was to call His disciples to prayer. "Pray ye therefore the Lord of the harvest, that he will send forth labourers into his harvest."

I find this very enlightening. Jesus is revealing His strategy to reach the world. Every God-initiated plan begins with prayer. There are many good scriptural prayers that we could pray, but when Jesus saw the needs of a sighing, dying, crying humanity, He called for one prayer. He said, "Pray for laborers!"

He did not tell them to pray for psychologists. He did not say to pray for social justice. He did not say to pray for an overthrow of the political system. He did not say to pray for the economy or the health care system. He did not even tell them to pray against the devil or against the spiritual forces in that region. When Jesus saw the scattered sheep, He said to pray for somebody who is willing to do some work, somebody who will preach some Gospel. Pray for somebody that's got some get-up-and-go to get with the program and take the Gospel to the world.

This is the great need. Workers! Workers! Workers! Workers to go! It is estimated that 41.2 percent of the world's population have never heard the Gospel message. (Source: The Joshua Project) Workers! Workers! Workers! Workers are needed!

When I was a growing up back in the '50s, there was a program on TV called The Dobie Gillis Show. Dobie had a friend named Maynard G. Krebs. Maynard was a "beatnik," kind of a precursor to the hippies of the '60s and '70s. One of Maynard's common traits was that anytime someone would use the word "work," Maynard would cry out with great fear and trepidation, "Work!!!" I think this is the way we are sometimes in the church. We are afraid of work. Oh, we may be willing to work for a paycheck or to further our career, but when it comes to working for the Lord, people want to leave that to the "professionals," the clergy. The truth is that we need a deep change of heart.

He said to pray that the Lord of the harvest would send laborers. You see, God must speak to your heart, and you must listen and respond. When this happens you will be changed. He will inspire you. He will empower you. Lives will be changed. Nations will be changed. When you hear and obey the calling voice of God, there will be miraculous results.

God's method has always been to send someone to do His work. Moses' ministry began at the burning bush when God sent him to deliver the people. Isaiah saw the Lord high and lifted up. He heard His voice saying, "Whom shall I send, and who will go for us? Then said I, Here am I; send me." Isaiah 6:8, KJV. The Apostle Paul was sent by Jesus Christ to the Gentiles "to open their eyes, and to turn them from darkness to light." Acts 26:18, KJV.

"Pray the Lord of the harvest." Pray for somebody to hear the call and to go. God's plan is always to use a man or a woman to accomplish His purposes. He uses people to reach people. It's about somebody who knows God telling someone else about Him. Freely you have received, freely give.

Jesus told His disciples, "Pray ye therefore the Lord of the harvest, that he will send forth labourers into his harvest." Before prayer changes things, prayer changes us. Jesus was looking for a heart change in His followers, so He told them to pray. He knew that they did not yet have His compassion for a lost humanity. They did not feel nor comprehend the deep need in the people's lives for the Good Shepherd. Only after their hearts were changed were they sent to the harvest fields.

The harvest is God's business. He is the Farm Boss. It is His heart, His passion. We must receive our marching orders from Him and "Go!" We must hear the call from the Father. We must hear God say "Go!" Then we can say like Isaiah, "Here am I, Lord, send me." He's the Lord of the harvest. He's the Farm Boss. We are the workers. "Pray the Lord of the harvest that He would send laborers."

Praying for All Men

"I exhort therefore, that, first of all, supplications, prayers, intercessions, and giving of thanks, be made for all men; For kings, and for all that are in authority; that we may lead a quiet and peaceable life in all godliness and honesty. For this is good and acceptable in the sight of God our Saviour; Who will have all men to be saved, and to come unto the knowledge of the truth. For there is one God, and one mediator between God and men, the man Christ Jesus; Who gave himself a ransom for all, to be testified in due time." 1 Timothy 2:1-6, KJV.

I have found that praying the Scriptures will change your heart. I have prayed this passage in Timothy many times. He says that first of all, prayers should be made for all men, not just for your family or friends or those in your church. Our priority in prayer should not be on "me, myself and I" or "us four, no more." No, we should be praying for the lost and scattered citizens of planet earth. And what should we pray? We should pray the will of God. And what is that will? That every one of them would be saved and come into the knowledge of the truth.

There is only one God! He is the God of Abraham, Isaac, and Jacob, and He is the Father of our Lord Jesus Christ. There is only one path to God. There is only one mediator and only one way to know God. His name is Jesus! No one can go to heaven without Him. He gave Himself as a ransom for all—for Hindus, for Muslims, for Buddhists, for atheists, and for God-haters. He died for them all.

The one thing that is missing is that we tell them what He has done for them. It is now due time for you and I to take that message to the world. As we pray, our hearts will be turned to a lost and dying world. Our apathy, complacency, and fear will be replaced by a holy zeal to see this world come to Jesus.

When we focus our prayers on the needs of the lost, it will change us, and it will ultimately change the world. It will continue that redemptive work which God planned from the foundation of the world and was consummated at the cross of Calvary and is now being proclaimed throughout the world. This should be our highest priority. This is a prayer that will revolutionize our lives and ministries.

That They Might Be Saved

Brethren, my heart's desire and prayer to God for Israel is, that they might be saved. (Romans 10:1, KJV).

We can feel with Paul this spiritual inner yearning, this burden "that they might be saved." He prayed for his countrymen "that they might be saved." He might have prayed for their prosperity or for peace from their enemies or something else, but his deepest heart's cry for them was "that they might be saved." Paul was saying that Israel needed to be be saved from the power and the penalty of sin through Jesus Christ. They were religious, but they had rejected the Savior. Therefore, they needed to be saved.

32

In an intercessory prayer meeting at a church where I was pastor, we were praying for our nation and the world, and this phrase kept coming up out of my spirit: "that they might be saved."

As we prayed for people in the media, I prayed "that they might be saved."

As we prayed for government officials, I prayed "that they might be saved."

As we prayed for church people who had no relationship with God, I prayed "that they might be saved."

As we prayed for the people in the Muslim nations, I prayed "that they might be saved."

As we prayed for the hurting, I prayed "that they might be saved."

This is the heart of God, "that they might be saved." As we give ourselves to prayer, that heart will be birthed in us and change will come. We must recognize the need for every human on the face of the earth to be rescued. The desire of God's heart, which He wants manifested through us in our prayers, our lifestyle, and our witness, is for the lost to be saved.

When our hearts are turned to God, we will feel the emptiness and pain of those all around us who are lost and without hope. Although as Christians we are a people of joy, we will feel the sadness of those around us who are away from God.

Weep for the Lost

"He that goeth forth and weepeth, bearing precious seed, shall doubtless come again with rejoicing, bringing his sheaves with him." Psalms 126:6, KJV.

Weeping is an entirely appropriate emotion in light of the spiritual and physical needs around us. I don't believe that we should allow the sorrow of the world to overtake us, but there is a godly sorrow which is normal for a believer who becomes aware of the needs of a lost and dying world.

When farmers would go out into the fields in the past, they would be "bearing precious seed." The seed that they were planting in the ground was also suitable for food for their families. They planted the seed at great personal cost. They would weep, knowing that they would not receive a return for several months.

And as we weep for souls, there is an emotional expenditure, a pouring out of one's heart for the needs of others. Likewise, planting the Gospel seed in the earth involves personal sacrifice. There are sacrifices such as the loss of comfort to take the Gospel to a foreign land, the giving of resources, and the risk of persecution. But as we sow those seeds of the heart, like the farmer, we will come again rejoicing, bringing our sheaves with us.

Intercessory prayer can be an intense activity, but can produce tremendous fruit. A farmer friend of mine from North Dakota was driving to town on an errand one day when the Lord spoke to him to go visit one of his neighbors. In obedience, he turned his truck around and drove to the man's house. This man's son had attempted suicide and was in the hospital. As my friend began to pray for his neighbor's son, the Holy Spirit took over, and he began to bow down and travail in prayer. He described it "like a woman giving birth." Now I can attest to you that this was not a normal thing for this reserved farmer from North Dakota. He told me that he had never experienced anything like that before. But within a few days, changes came to the young man who had attempted suicide. He gave his life to Jesus and began to hunger for the Word of God with a desire to become a dedicated follower of Jesus Christ.

When God grips your heart for the lost, there will be a change both in you and in the world around you. I'm convinced that we have yet to see the full potential of the release of God's power as we give ourselves to prayer for a lost and dying world. You can touch the world through prayer!

Father, all around me are lost souls. They are scattered like sheep without a shepherd. They need You Lord. You want everyone to be saved and come to the knowledge of the truth. There's only one way to come to You. There's only one mediator, Your Son Jesus Christ. Father, send laborers into Your harvest fields. Speak to men and women and boys and girls to share the love of Jesus with those around them, so that the people might come back to You, in Jesus' name I pray. Amen.

Chapter 5

Keep Your Eyes on the Prize

"In the mean while his disciples prayed him, saying, Master, eat. But he said unto them, I have meat to eat that ye know not of. Therefore said the disciples one to another, Hath any man brought him ought to eat? Jesus saith unto them, My meat is to do the will of him that sent me, and to finish his work. Say not ye, There are yet four months, and then cometh harvest? behold, I say unto you, Lift up your eyes, and look on the fields; for they are white already to harvest." John 4:31-35, KJV.

All around our home in southern Minnesota lie massive fields of corn and soybeans. At harvest time there is a tremendous amount of energy that goes into getting the crop into the bins. The focus is all on the harvest.

When my neighbor harvests his fields, he brings in a small army to help him. They set up a base of operations on the edge of the field. Pick-up trucks converge and tractors appear, towing huge gravity boxes. Then there are usually a couple of combines and a semitrailer in which to load the grain. Everyone is focused on the same goal—bringing in the harvest. They're not taking time out to watch the World Series or to analyze the fertilizer program for the next year. They're not doing maintenance on their houses, sheds, or grain bins. It's harvest time, and it's everyone's business to bring it in.

Before harvest time, there is focus too. The preparation of the soil, the planting of the seed, the fertilizer, and the weed program are all about the harvest. That's the bottom line. As the crop is growing, it's being nurtured and protected. The equipment is being prepared. Plans are being made. After all, what's the use of farming if there is no harvest?

Once my neighbor and his team were working all night to bring in a field of corn across the highway from my place. Nothing distracted them. The crops were ripe and the weather was about to change. Snow was predicted. It was time to get the crop in the bins. Everyone shared in the essential task at hand, and no doubt everyone shared in the benefits of the harvest.

Like my neighbor, Jesus is focused on reaping a ripe harvest. And He wants you and me to team up with Him in the great cause of His life—the harvest. The harvest is people—people who need the Lord, the people you are rubbing elbows with in your daily life—your neighbor, the elderly man you take care of each day, the customer you serve, the rancher from South Dakota, the goat herder in Kenya, the artist in New York City, the day laborer in India, the shopkeeper in eastern Europe, the business person, the airline stewardess on your flight. All around the world, people need the Lord!

Jesus longed to impart His Father's will to His disciples. Don't say, "Let's wait four months"—later, later, later. Look! The fields are ripe now. If you don't harvest the crop, it will be lost forever. He was never unclear about His mission. His purpose has not changed. Now He is working through you and me.

How often have you gotten your eyes upon something else other than the harvest? How often have you been seeking satisfaction in some worldly attraction or even a religious thing and forgotten what is important to the Father? Jesus never lost sight of why He was here on earth. He never deviated from His true purpose. "The Son of man," He said, "is sent to seek and to save the lost." Likewise, we in His Church have been given this same mission. We are to bring the Father's children home. As John Wesley said to the preachers working under him, "You have one business on earth—to save souls."

In the natural world, we are told to keep our eyes on the road, because if we are looking at the ditch, we may end up there. Jesus was giving His disciples the secret of effective evangelism. "Look on the fields, for they are white unto harvest." He didn't say, "Look at the problems in your life or in the Church." He didn't say, "Look at the economy." He didn't say, "Look at the circumstances around you." No, these are things that keep us from the goal. They are diversions. He said, "Keep your eyes on the ripe fields."

Whatever you fix your eyes on is the direction you are going. It is your goal and your passion, the thing that consumes your energy. Jesus said, "Say not ye, There are yet four months, and then cometh harvest? behold, I say unto you, Lift up your eyes, and look on the fields; for they are white already to harvest." John 4:35, KJV.

All around us are spiritually destitute people—people who need Jesus in their lives. Yet we hardly notice. Why? Because our eyes are on other things. We are looking at our bank account, our career, our ministries, our personal needs. We are following after conspiracy theories or the "latest revelation." Our eyes are on the problems of the world, on political controversies and trivialities. But Jesus said, "Keep your eyes on the fields." (author's paraphrase) Why? Because they are ready. They are ripe!

There is no lack of candidates for salvation. There is no lack of people ready to receive Jesus. The only lack is for laborers, workers for the harvest fields of this world. The laborers are few, because they are distracted. Our focus and our vision is everything. We must see the needs and seize the opportunities. We must have spiritual vision that lines up with the will of the Father. Keep your eyes on the prize!

When we align our hearts with the heart of the Father and begin to do His will, then we will find the true joy of the Christian life. As we take our eyes off ourselves and off of Christian personalities, denominations, and movements, and begin to look at the ripe fields, we will regain a sense of purpose and meaning and true stability that will sustain us in the journey of life. As we act on what we are seeing by reaching out to lost, needy, and hurting people, we will find the true joy of the Christian life, because true joy is obtained not only in finding Jesus, but also in giving Him away.

Many church members today are dissatisfied with the Christian life and wonder why. All the latest Christian CDs, t-shirts, and shallow church services leave them empty and looking for something more. So they look further for a new teaching, a fresh understanding of the Word of God that will excite them and stimulate their faith. Tired and frustrated church leaders look for some new program or idea that will excite their people, but what people need is to a receive a challenge that will move them to action and ultimately fill the deepest need of their hearts.

When Jesus told His disciples, "I have meat that you know not of," He was telling them that He had something in His life that satisfied Him more than the finest cuisine of the most expensive restaurant in all of Israel. He was saying, "My meat, my passion, the thing that really sustains and drives me, is to do the will of My Father and finish it." Jesus lived a purpose-filled life. He was motivated by the will of God, and He stretched out with all His being to accomplish His Father's objective.

Today we have a lot of programs, teachings, movements, and fads which distract us from the real purpose of the Church, which is to reach the world. These are not all necessarily bad things. But sometimes good things can be the enemy of the God thing. Oswald Smith, the great missionary pastor from Toronto, Canada, said, "Oh my friends, we are loaded with countless church activities, while the real work of the church, that of evangelizing and winning the lost is almost entirely neglected."

Our message is "Jesus Christ and Him crucified." This is why Jesus came and why His Church exists, to save sinners like you and me. As the Apostle Paul said, "This is a faithful saying, and worthy of all acceptation, that Christ Jesus came into the world to save sinners; of whom I am chief." 1 Timothy 1:15, KJV. The clear teaching of the Word of God is that without Jesus Christ we are all without hope and without God and headed for an eternity of torment in the fires of hell. Judgment is sure for all of us and much deserved, because all of us have sinned and come short of the glory of God. (Rom. 3:23)

We're on a Rescue Mission

"And it came to pass, that the beggar died, and was carried by the angels into Abraham's bosom: the rich man also died, and was buried; And in hell he lift up his eyes, being in torments, and seeth Abraham afar off, and Lazarus in his bosom. And he cried and said, Father Abraham, have mercy on me, and send Lazarus, that he

may dip the tip of his finger in water, and cool my tongue; for I am tormented in this flame." Luke 16:22-24, KJV.

Jesus told the story of the rich man and Lazarus. The rich man cried out in torment in the flames of hell. Can you imagine what it would be like to go out into eternity without hope and without God, to face an eternity of judgment in the fires of hell? Would you wish a future like that for anyone?

The rich man didn't go to hell because he was rich, but because his priorities were wrong. He was not rich toward God. His carelessness and selfishness cost him dearly. Many people are in the same position today.

In the natural world, when someone is caught in a burning building, we don't leave them there to die in the flames. We do all we can to rescue them. On September 11, 2001, a total of 403 firefighters, paramedics, and police offices died trying to rescue people from the burning remains of the Twin Towers in New York City. They literally gave their lives to rescue others from the inferno. Jesus came to rescue those who are heading for a certain destruction in the fires of hell. And He calls us to join Him in that mission.

Preaching on hell has become unpopular in our day, but the Word of God never changes, regardless of the opinions of man. Jesus spoke more about hell than any other preacher in the Bible. The terror of an eternity separate from God was very real to Him.

There is a hell, and no one in their right mind would want to go there. But God in His love and mercy has made the way for us to be forgiven and to receive the gift of eternal life.

It is not the will of God that anyone should suffer in Hell. Hell is a place prepared for the devil and his angels. God's will is that everyone should be saved from the awful judgment of hell. "The Lord is not slack concerning his promise, as some men count slackness; but is longsuffering to us-ward, not willing that any should perish, but that all should come to repentance." 2 Peter 3:9, KJV.

The Bible says, "And as it is appointed unto men once to die, but after this the judgment:" Hebrews 9:27, KJV. There is no reincarnation. There is no purgatory. There is no second chance. Yet today, 40 percent of the world's population have not heard the message of His gift of eternal life. They have not heard for one reason—we have not told them. We have not completed our mission.

When I look around the world and see the various endeavors of men, I see courage, commitment, and resolve. In the rescue workers in New York and the military personnel around the world, for example, I see a determined purpose and great sense of mission. Even in the business world and sports arena, I see men and women of courage, determination, and resolve, who are willing to sacrifice all for their cause.

How much more should we be faithful to our Lord in reaching out to a lost and dying world, to rescue them from a sure and fiery hell? Evangelism involves sacrifice. It can mean being away from home and family. It can mean suffering ridicule from co-workers and friends. It can even mean risking your life. But for those who are willing to take the challenge, the rewards are great. As Jesus said, "For whosoever will save his life shall lose it: but whosoever will lose his life for my sake, the same shall save it." Luke 9:24, KJV. Do you want to really come alive? Lay down your life for Jesus!

General William Booth, founder of the Salvation Army said, "You have enjoyed yourself in Messiahianity long enough. You have had pleasant feelings, pleasant songs, pleasant meetings, pleasant prospects. There has been much of human happiness, much clapping of hands, and much shouting of praises—very much of heaven on earth. Now then, go to God and tell Him you are prepared as much as necessary to turn your back upon it all, and that you are willing to spend the rest of your days struggling in the midst of perishing multitudes, whatever it may cost you."

When Jesus walked this earth, He was passionate about His mission and purpose. " For the Son of man is come to seek and to save that which was lost." Luke 19:10, KJV. Jesus had a clear mission, and everything else was built around that. When He called the disciples, His purpose was to reach the lost. When He taught the Sermon on the Mount,

His purpose was to reach the lost. When He went to the cross, His purpose was to reach the lost. He came to seek and save the lost. This is the heartbeat of the Father, then and now. Nothing has changed. The Father is looking for His children to come home.

Today, you and I also are strategically placed on this earth "to seek and save the lost." That is our purpose. That is our mission. Everything points to it. This is God's direction for our lives. Before He left the earth, Jesus told His disciples, "Go ye into all the world, and preach the gospel to every creature. He that believeth and is baptized shall be saved; but he that believeth not shall be damned." Mark 16:15, 16, KJV.

This was Jesus' final message to His followers. "Touch the world for Me," says the Lord.

Dear Father, give me Your heart for a lost and dying world. Help me to keep my eyes on the harvest, and to make it my business to bring in the harvest, in Jesus' name. Amen.

Chapter 6

You Can Share Jesus

"And all things are of God, who hath reconciled us to himself by Jesus Christ, and hath given to us the ministry of reconciliation;" 2 Corinthians 5:18, KJV.

When Jesus is in your life, you have something to share with those around you. You can share your testimony about what Jesus has done for you. You can share His love. That is what it means to be a witness. Your life and your testimony are some of the most powerful tools you have to share with others. It doesn't matter if you came from a down-in-the-gutter background or if you were a "goody two shoes." Your testimony matters and is powerful. It's an example of what God can do in a person's life.

Research consistently shows that between 80 to 90 percent of the people that come to Christ come as the result of the witness or the invitation of a friend or relative. Without common everyday believers reaching out to their friends, neighbors, and relatives, the work of the Church is quite ineffective. It's your personal witness that makes a difference in your community and in the world.

Unlike a sermon, when you are sharing Christ one-on-one, you are not giving a speech, but you are talking *with* someone. You are cultivating a relationship, listening to them, asking about their lives, and sharing back and forth. By being a friend and caring about them personally, you earn the right to share with them about your hope in Jesus. Then sharing what God has done in your life comes much more naturally.

Also, remember that actions speak louder than words. So, live your life as an example before the people around you. Let them see Jesus in the way that you do business and handle your relationships. Let them see Jesus in the way you treat your spouse and the way you talk about others. Be guided by the love of God. Mahatma Gandhi is quoted as saying, "I like your Christ. I do not like your Christians." By the grace of God, let's endeavor to accurately represent our Lord as faithful ambassadors. "Now then we are ambassadors for Christ, as though God did beseech you by us: we pray you in Christ's stead, be ye reconciled to God." 2 Corinthians 5:20, KJV.

As you grow as a disciple of Christ, make it your goal to learn how to share the message of the Gospel with others. Imagine your neighbor coming to you today and asking the question, "How can I find eternal life?" Do you have the answer? Could you explain to him the plan of salvation and tell them how to receive Jesus Christ as his personal Lord and Savior? As Charles Spurgeon said, "We must school and train ourselves to deal personally with the unconverted. We must not excuse ourselves, but force ourselves to the irksome task until it becomes easy."

Don't be discouraged about what you don't know, but make it a priority to progressively increase in your ability to share Christ. If you had a new job that involved unfamiliar tasks, you would make it your business to perfect the skills needed to satisfy your employer. Honor our Father as much as you would an earthly supervisor. Learn the skills necessary to accomplish your mission in life. Satisfaction comes only as you place yourself in the center of God's will.

Pray for God's help in being a witness for Him. This is a prayer that He will answer. Someone once suggested the following prayer to use when an opportunity comes to share Christ with someone: "Lord, open the door. Open their heart. Open my mouth."

Ask your Father for boldness. When the early church was persecuted, they asked God for boldness rather than a place to hide. "And now, Lord, behold their threatenings: and grant unto thy servants, that with all boldness they may speak thy word, By stretching forth thine hand to heal; and that signs and wonders may be done by the name of thy holy child Jesus. And when they had prayed, the place was shaken where they were assembled together; and they were all filled with the Holy Ghost, and they spake the word of God with boldness." Acts 4:29-31, KJV. If you want God to "shake up" your life and your church, pray for boldness to speak God's Word. You will be amazed by the results, because this is a prayer that is according to His will.

As you're rubbing shoulders with people in the grocery store, at school, in your community, even in your home, you will find that the people around you have great needs. They need healing. They need peace. They need wisdom. God has all these good things, and He lives in you. When someone around you is hurting, just reach over and touch them and say a simple prayer. It doesn't have to be anything formal. Just say, "Dear Father, You see my friend Jack and the need that is in his life. Touch him right now by the power of Your Spirit and heal him. Help him through this trial in his life. Give him peace, in Jesus' name I pray." Often when you pray that type of prayer, a person's heart will melt and open up to the message you have for them. Pray for people. Be a "need-meeter" and look for those open doors to share the love of God.

If you attend a church that is focused on preaching the Gospel and making disciples, one of the best things that you can do is to invite your friends, relatives, coworkers, and the people that you meet to come to church with you. Remember that you are not alone. The church is to be like a family, inviting guests over for dinner. A national survey by the Barna Group found that one out of four unchurched people said that they would gladly attend church if a friend would only extend an invitation. As a witness for Christ, I encourage you to work with your local church. Tell people about Jesus. Tell them what He has done in your life. Bring them to church, where they can be taught the Word of God and learn to become a disciple of Christ. As we work together, we will bring in the harvest in these last days.

The story is told about a shopkeeper in London who became convicted about the need to share Christ. He made a commitment to take a half an hour out of each day to reach out to others. Each day at a certain time, he would pray, walk out the door of his shop, and hand Gospel tracts to the people passing by. For many years he followed this pattern. He never knew if anyone had been reached through his actions. Some time later, the story goes, a missionary was giving his testimony at a ministers conference and shared about how a man had given him a tract and he had found Christ and later became a minister of the Gospel. The surprising thing was that many other ministers at the same conference also testified that they had been touched by the simple obedience of that same London shopkeeper.

I have heard some people criticize the use of Gospel tracts as a means of witnessing by saying that a person's verbal witness is much more effective. However, I believe that God can use whatever act of obedience that we are capable of accomplishing. Something is *much* better than nothing. Sometimes passing out a tract can be a first step towards verbal witness. It puts into action the law of inertia which states that an object in motion tends to stay in motion. Get moving for Jesus and watch for the results.

I have personally observed the success of Gospel tracts in reaching the lost. A young man named Steve walked into a church that I was pastoring. Someone had given him a Gospel tract while he was living in another state. The title read, "How Hot is Hell?" He immediately threw the tract away, but that title stuck with him. When he moved to our town he was looking for a a place to learn more about Jesus and ended up at our church. He looked something like I did before I came to Jesus. But the people of the church loved him and we encouraged him and taught him the Word of God. He became a very diligent follower of Christ, was mightily transformed, and later became a minister of the Gospel. So, I say, "Praise God for tracts!" Here's Steve's testimony in his own words:

I was living in Las Vegas with an old buddy from when I was in the Air Force. I had a serious problem with drugs and alcohol. I was employed with Manpower (a temp service), and they would send me to various construction sites to do grunt work. I did not have a car at the time, so I had to get up REALLY early to hoof my way to whatever job I was being assigned to. One morning I had to walk through the main strip of Vegas. As I was walking down the street, a middle-aged woman handed me a tract with a question on the cover, "How Hot is Hell?" After reading the title I promptly threw the tract away. The funny thing, however, is that those words stuck in my head. I would be working as a laborer on a job site in the hot Nevada sun, and being a midwest boy, I was not used to the heat. I would be sweating and

52

thinking, "Man this is hot," and then I would hear a little voice inside my head saying, "You haven't even seen hot yet—just wait 'til you go to hell."

At the time I was not sure what to think about God, I was not even convinced that there was a God, heaven, hell, etc. However, I was haunted with the whole notion of going to hell after my brief "encounter" with that tract. The whole idea was alarming enough that I decided I had better look into it further. I figured that if there really was a hell, chances were really good that is where I was going to end up. I picked up a New Testament in a used book store and began to pour over it. I was absolutely struck with the person of Jesus. Everything that He said carried authority and rang true. Even though I really didn't understand it very well, I began to realize that I was on to something very "big!" That New Testament also had a "sinners prayer" in the back. I made sure that I prayed it almost daily. So that is how the first steps of the journey began.

My roommate in Vegas had all kinds of lab equipment in the house for cooking up drugs and we had reason to believe that the house was being watched. I decided it was time to split, and I moved to Minnesota where I had a friend who had invited me to come and live and look for work. I eventually ended up in Howard Lake. I was still pretty tangled up with drugs. One Sunday morning after I had been up all night partying, I decided to walk down to the corner store and grab a Mountain Dew to wake me up a bit. As I walked by that "MTV Church" with the satellite up on the roof (Solid Rock Church!!!) I got a bit of a wild idea in my head and decided to go in

53

and check it out. I walked into the middle of the praise and worship time with people clapping their hands and raising their hands and such, some "really heavy religion in progress." After the worship was a greeting time, and I think somehow word got around that "We've got us one here in the back." Everyone was shaking my hand or hugging me. I was quite uncomfortable, but everyone seemed very genuine and that really impressed me. After that, the journey began in earnest.

Don't Be Ruled by Your Fears

It's best to be natural, comfortable, and relaxed as you share the Gospel. However, if you can't be relaxed and comfortable, share the Gospel anyway. The power is not in your disposition, but in the Gospel itself. I love to tell the story of a man named Edward Kimble, who shared his faith with a shoe salesman many years ago.

"It was July 1, 1885 when Edward Kimble felt the tugging of the Spirit to share his faith with a young shoe salesman he knew. At first Kimble vacillated, unsure if he should talk to the man. But he finally mustered his courage and went into the shoe store. There Kimble found the salesman in the back room stocking shoes, and he began to share his faith with him. As a result, the young shoe salesman prayed and received Jesus Christ that day. That shoe salesman's name was Dwight L. Moody, and he became the greatest evangelist of his generation." (Source: Tree of Life Bible Church website)

Edward Kimble's nervous attempt to share his faith is still bearing much fruit today, as the influence of the Gospel that D.L. Moody preached is still multiplying in the earth. In fact, Billy Graham and many others can trace their spiritual genealogy back to D.L. Moody. Aren't you glad that Edward Kimble obeyed God and witnessed to that shoe salesman?

When I am speaking to a person and looking for an opportunity to share, I am at the same time asking God to give me the key to their heart. The Lord will sometimes give me a word of knowledge about their situation that will open the door wide for a discussion of spiritual things. Once the subject of the conversation is on spiritual things, I can begin to share the Gospel message.

The Apostle Paul said, "For I am not ashamed of the gospel of Christ: for it is the power of God unto salvation to every one that believeth; to the Jew first, and also to the Greek." Romans 1:16, KJV. It's the Gospel that is the power of salvation, not a church creed or religious ritual. It's not even Bible teaching about how to live the Christian life. These things are for people who have already received Christ. Sometimes we make the mistake of trying to make someone into a disciple of Christ before they have heard the Gospel and made a commitment to follow Jesus.

The Gospel is simple. Jesus died for your sins. He was buried. He rose again. By receiving Him as Savior and the Lord of your life, you can become a child of God. This is the message that we need to bring to people, so that they may be saved. "For I delivered unto you first of all that which I also received, how that Christ died for our sins according to the scriptures; And that he was buried, and that he rose again the third day according to the scriptures:" 1 Corinthians 15:3, 4, KJV.

Here are some tips for sharing the Gospel one-on-one:

- Resist intimidation. You have Good News to share. Take an attitude of love, genuine concern, and boldness.

- Ask questions about the person's life and interests. Let them know by listening that you care about them.

- Do not try to correct them for wrong attitudes, ideas, etc. If they don't know Jesus, they are just acting normal.

- Remember you are presenting a Person, not just a doctrine.

- Stress the love of God. The Lord is merciful and kind and has made a way for everyone to receive His free gift of salvation. There is an eternal judgment, but it is not God's will for anyone.

- Keep it simple—one God, one Savior, one cross, one salvation. The person you are sharing with does not need a theological treatise. The simple Gospel works best.

- Give them and opportunity to respond to the Gospel you present. If they don't, keep the door open and the friendship viable.

Basic Principles for Sharing the Gospel

Here is a basic summary of principles that are used by many people and organizations for sharing the Gospel. You can find these principles in an illustrated Gospel tract from the Billy Graham Evangelistic Association called *Steps to Peace with God*. You can order these tracts and use them as a guide for witnessing. You can also memorize these points and share them from your heart.

I have used the *Steps to Peace with God* booklet as a guide to share Christ with people that I meet. The illustrations make it easy to explain the concept of the Gospel and God's plan of salvation. I can also leave the tract with the person so they can go over it later when they are alone. This way, if they don't receive Christ immediately, the Holy Spirit has another chance later to speak to their heart. If they do receive Christ, the booklet serves as a reminder of their decision and of the need to take the next steps in their walk with God.

As the basic principles become embedded in your heart as a witness, you can use them even if you don't have the booklet along. You can draw the illustrations on a napkin at a restaurant, for example, and write down the Scripture references or just share the basic truths of the Gospel from your heart. You will have to find what method works best for you in sharing the Gospel.

Sometimes there are barriers to communication that make it seem impossible to share Christ with others, but the Holy Spirit knows how to bridge those gaps and make communication possible. I once shared the Gospel with a young Chinese woman in an airport, while I was waiting for a flight. She knew very little English, so I drew illustrations on a scrap of paper to demonstrate the work of the cross to bridge the gap between God and man. She also had a small electronic device, which translated words from English into her language. I used that device to explain the Gospel through basic words, such as forgiveness, substitution, reconciliation, and redemption. Just before I got on my plane this woman received Christ in prayer. As I walked away, she was weeping for joy. That's the power of the Gospel of Jesus Christ.

Here are four basic principles and some scriptures that relate to each of them:

Step #1 God's Plan: Peace and Life

God loves you. His plan for you is salvation and for you to enjoy all His blessings. God doesn't want anyone to suffer in hell, but for all to have eternal life with Him.

"And God said, Let us make man in our image, after our likeness: and let them have dominion over the fish of the sea, and over the fowl of the air, and over the cattle, and over all the earth, and over every creeping thing that creepeth upon the earth. So God created man in his own image, in the image of God created he him; male and female created he them. And God blessed them, and God said unto them, Be fruitful, and multiply, and replenish the earth, and subdue it: and have dominion over the fish of the sea, and over the fowl of the air, and over every living thing that moveth upon the earth." Genesis 1:26-28, KJV.

"The thief cometh not, but for to steal, and to kill, and to destroy: I am come that they might have life, and that they might have it more abundantly." John 10:10, KJV.

Step #2 The Problem: Our Separation

Although God wants to save everyone, He cannot tolerate sin. He is a holy God and will not live with sin, and He will judge sin. Everyone has sinned. Therefore, everyone is condemned and without Christ and will suffer eternal damnation. Those who die without Christ will go to a place of fire and torment called hell. The Bible teaches that at the end of the age, death and hell and everyone whose name is not written in the Lamb's Book of Life will be cast into a place of everlasting punishment called the lake of fire, where they will spend eternity with the devil.

"For all have sinned, and come short of the glory of God;" Romans 3:23, KJV.

"Wherefore, as by one man sin entered into the world, and death by sin; and so death passed upon all men, for that all have sinned:" Romans 5:12, KJV.

"For the wages of sin is death; but the gift of God is eternal life through Jesus Christ our Lord." Romans 6:23, KJV.

Step #3 God's Bridge: The Cross

Because of His love, God sent His Son Jesus Christ to die for our sins, and to deliver us from eternal damnation. He was born of a virgin, lived a sinless life, died for our sins on the cross, was buried, and rose from the dead. He was God in the flesh, and now is our living Lord.

"But God commendeth his love toward us, in that, while we were yet sinners, Christ died for us." Romans 5:8, KJV.

"For God so loved the world, that he gave his only begotten Son, that whosoever believeth in him should not perish, but have everlasting life." John 3:16, KJV.

"Jesus saith unto him, I am the way, the truth, and the life: no man cometh unto the Father, but by me." John 14:6, KJV.

Step #4 Our Response: Receive Christ

By receiving Christ as our personal Lord and Savior, we are set free from the judgment and the power of sin. We must make a decision in our heart to turn from sin and unto God and to trust Jesus for our salvation. As a gift from God, we are given eternal life and become children of God.

"But as many as received him, to them gave he power to become the sons of God, even to them that believe on his name:" John 1:12, KJV.

"That if thou shalt confess with thy mouth the Lord Jesus, and shalt believe in thine heart that God hath raised him from the dead, thou shalt be saved. For with the heart man believeth unto righteousness; and with the mouth confession is made unto salvation." Romans 10:9, 10, KJV.

"Behold, I stand at the door, and knock: if any man hear my voice, and open the door, I will come in to him, and will sup with him, and he with me." Revelation 3:20, KJV.

Jesus Christ is standing at the doorway of your heart, wanting to come in and live in your heart. Would you like to receive Him today as your Lord and Savior? Pray this prayer from your heart:

Dear God, I admit I am a sinner. Without Christ I am lost. But I thank You that You sent Jesus Christ, Your Son, to die for my sins. I believe You raised Him from the dead. I receive Jesus Christ as my Lord and Savior. I turn away from every sin and choose to follow You. Thank You for saving me. I believe that I am a child of God and that I can call You Father, in Jesus' name. Amen.

Chapter 7

Lifestyle Evangelism

"But ye shall receive power, after that the Holy Ghost is come upon you: and ye shall be witnesses unto me both in Jerusalem, and in all Judaea, and in Samaria, and unto the uttermost part of the earth." Acts 1:8, KJV.

Back in the '70s, I met a man working at a sawmill where I was employed in southeast Minnesota. He was not a pastor or a preacher, just an ordinary worker like me, but he loved the Lord. He would talk to me about his church, a small fellowship of "Spirit-filled" Christians. "How do you know they are Spirit-filled?" I would tease him. He was always asking me to come to his church. Meanwhile, he was living the Christian life before me and sharing stories about what God had done in his life.

One night, he invited me, my wife, and our baby daughter Heidi for dinner at his home. His wife prepared a good meal. They both were warm and friendly, and they shared about some of the things that God had done in their lives. Like many of us at that time, they had come out of the long-haired hippie drug culture, but their lives had been transformed by the power of God. Once again that night, they invited us to visit their church. An evangelist was in town, and we should come, they said. Now, since they had been so nice to us, we felt obligated.

At the meeting, all the Christians (mostly young 20-somethings like ourselves) were singing lively Scripture choruses, jumping and shouting and praising God. We saw that God was real in their lives. During that meeting, my friend who had invited me went forward for prayer. He had suffered from Rheumatic Fever as a child and as a result had a deformity in one of the valves in his heart. After receiving prayer, he began to shout at the top of his lungs, "Hallelujah!" Then he testified that God had touched his heart, and he knew that he was healed.

The next day after the meeting, he went to the doctor and it was confirmed that he had been healed of the problem. Coincidentally, it seemed, I was the first person to see him after he left the doctor's office and to hear the report of his miraculous healing. The doctor said that the heart murmur which he had before was nearly gone and his blood pressure was normal, a huge change. Several weeks later, he was at the doctor's office once again and was told that the heart murmur was completely gone. That experience had a tremendous impact on our lives.

During the meeting with the evangelist, something had told me, "This is what you've been looking for." I had been searching for spiritual peace through drugs, transcendental meditation, and eastern mysticism, but suddenly I sensed that I had found something real. We didn't give our lives to Jesus that night, but a seed had been planted in our hearts. From that day, we never missed church. Within several months, both Susan and I surrendered our lives to Jesus and were water baptized.

We didn't look the best or even smell the best, but the people in that little church showed us kindness. The women in that church would come to visit my wife. They would teach her the Bible. "Let's open to the book of Ephesians," they would say. And she would thumb through the Bible searching for Ephesians. We didn't know much about the Bible, but we recognized the love of God in the people. That is what lifestyle evangelism is all about!

If we want to be successful reaching people for Christ, this is what we need to do. Sometimes Christians are so wrapped up in their own lives that they don't pay attention to the people around them or even those that visit the church. But, if we are really following Jesus, we should care for the people who come into our midst.

Worldwide, it is estimated that only one third of all born again Christians ever do anything about the Great Commission. The greatest potential for evangelism is not in the preachers, but in the people. This work of evangelism is done in the trenches, out where people live and work everyday. It's lifestyle evangelism, people reaching out to the people around them.

Think about it for a moment. If every Christian in the world would just win one person to the Lord per year and teach them to be disciples, then every year the Church would double, and before long we would reach the whole world for Jesus.

The Bible talks about five types of ministries which have been given by Jesus to develop His Church. "And he gave some, apostles; and some, prophets; and some, evangelists; and some, pastors and teachers; For the perfecting of the saints, for the work of the ministry, for the edifying of the body of Christ:" Ephesians 4:11, 12, KJV. These ministers are essential to God's Kingdom work, but the purpose of the apostles, prophets, evangelists, pastors, and teachers is to train God's people so that they might do their ministry of building up the Church. The amplified version of Ephesians 4:12 reads: "His intention was the perfecting and the full equipping of the saints (His consecrated people), [that they should do] the work of ministering toward building up Christ's Body (the Church)."

Preacher, it's not your job alone to win the whole world to Jesus. Your job is to equip God's people to do their job, which is to build up Christ's Body, the Church, and to reach the world for Christ. The people sitting in the pew are not just people to preach to; that's the army of the Lord sitting in front of you. You need to give them direction. You need to send them out to the field to be witnesses for the Lord. That's God's vision for the Body. That's what we are going to see in these last days.

66

Ordinary, everyday believers are called to reach out where they live and work, to be examples to the world around them, to encourage and help other believers, and to build the work of God in the earth. The Scripture says that we are all to be "fitly joined together and compacted (or knit together) by that which every joint supplieth." In other words, every person in Christ's Body, the Church, is essential for the full functioning of the Body. We are to be united together and working together for the common cause of reaching people for Jesus Christ. Every part is important. For example, in our natural bodies, even the loss or injury of one small part, such as a baby toe, can greatly hinder the functioning of the Body. As we all work together in relationship, we will see the work of God accomplished in the earth. You are needed!

In 1961, God gave a supernatural vision to American evangelist Tommy Hicks. The vision originally appeared in a book entitled *Pertinent Prophecies* by John N. and Dorothea M. Gardner. To summarize it briefly, God took him far above the earth. As he looked down, he could see the nations of the world, and the islands of the sea. Then, he saw a great giant which seemed to encompass the whole earth. The giant was covered in debris and choked with mud. The giant then began to raise his hands and worship the Lord. Then the giant seemed to melt into the earth and become rivulets of gold and silver all throughout the nations of the world. Then Hicks saw ordinary believers all over the world. He saw the Lord Jesus stretching His hands towards them, and a glory, which looked like liquid fire, coming out of His hands. Then these same ordinary believers began to stretch their hands and that same liquid fire began to flow and miracles began to take place all over the world. I'll share a portion of his prophecy here:

"I was bewildered as I watched it, but these people that he had anointed, hundreds of thousands of people all over the world, in Africa, England, Russia, China, America, all over the world, the anointing of God was upon these people as they went forward in the name of the Lord. I saw these men and women as they went forth. They were ditch diggers, they were washerwomen, they were rich men, they were poor men. I saw people who were bound with paralysis and sickness and blindness and deafness. As the Lord stretched forth to give them this anointing, they became well, they became healed, and they went forth!

"And this is the miracle of it—this is the glorious miracle of it—those people would stretch forth their hands exactly as the Lord did, and it seemed as if there was this same liquid fire in their hands. As they stretched forth their hands they said, 'According to my word, be thou made whole.'

"As these people continued in this mighty end-time ministry, I did not fully realize what it was, and I looked to the Lord and said, 'What is the meaning of this?' And He said, 'This is that which I will do in the last days. I will restore all that the cankerworm, the palmerworm, the

caterpiller—I will restore all that they have destroyed. This, my people, in the end times will go forth. As a mighty army shall they sweep over the face of the earth.'"

Jesus told the early believers that they would receive the power of the Holy Spirit in order to be witnesses "in all Judaea, and in Samaria, and unto the uttermost part of the earth." Notice they were to begin in Jerusalem, in their hometown, and spread out from there. God's plan is for the whole world. There are no limits. But God's plan for evangelism begins at home, right where you live.

How can we as Christians touch this world for God? We must be filled with the Spirit. Like the believers in Tommy Hicks' vision, we need to receive the "liquid fire" from Jesus. As we seek God and allow Him to permeate our lives, as we worship Him and live before Him, He will fill our hearts with His glory. Each day we need to cultivate the presence of God in our lives. The world needs Jesus Christ. Our job is to carry His presence to the people.

Jesus is no longer physically on the earth, but you are, and as a believer, you are the Body of Christ (the Anointed One). It's His anointing in you that will touch the world. As you carry that anointing to work, to the store, in your home, and in your daily life, Jesus will touch people all around you wherever you go. The Bible says we have this treasure in earthen vessels (in our physical bodies), that the excellency may be of God and not of us. (2 Cor. 4:7) That treasure is His glory, His presence, His anointing. This is a word, not only for ministers in the pulpit, but for the whole Body. "Be filled with the spirit." Every member of His Body should seek to be filled with the Spirit.

Jesus told His disciples, "For John truly baptized with water; but ye shall be baptized with the Holy Ghost not many days hence." Acts 1:5, KJV. There is a baptism (or immersion) with water, but there is also a baptism (immersion) with the Holy Spirit. The Spirit of God will come upon you and submerge you and He will empower you. Every believer has the Spirit of God in their life, but when Jesus baptizes you in the Holy Spirit, gifts of the Spirit will flow in your life to help you to touch the world for Jesus.

Spend time with God. Wait upon the Lord and His anointing will come upon your life. Ask Him to baptize you in the Holy Spirit. Everywhere you go, the Holy Spirit will go with you. You are called to be a portable walking temple for the Lord. When Peter walked down the street, the sick and those vexed with unclean spirits were healed. (Acts 5:15-16) Why did that happen? Because the glory of God was on his life. God is not limited. He will still do these things today through those who live in His presence and walk in His ways.

I want you to see this picture today for lifestyle evangelism—the Spirit of God moving in your life to reach everyone you touch. Be filled with the Spirit. Then the love of God will flow out of your life. Live in His presence and let His love flow out of you. Jesus said, "Out of your belly shall flow rivers of living water."

Lifestyle Evangelism Is All About Loving People

"As the Father hath loved me, so have I loved you: continue ye in my love." John 15:9, KJV.

You will notice in the ministry of Jesus, He loved people where they were at, unconditionally. The religious leaders were always criticizing Him for eating with the sinners and tax collectors. But that was the Jesus style. He loved the people. He fed them. He was kind to them and that opened their hearts to Him. That's what lifestyle evangelism is—like the couple that reached out to my wife and me and the people in that fellowship in southeastern Minnesota. That's how you break down the walls, with kindness. Love the people.

Sometimes Christians have the attitude, "Once they clean up their lives, then I will welcome them." That's not going to work. Jesus saw Zacchaeus up in a tree and He said, "Let's do lunch." So Jesus went to Zacchaeus' home and had lunch. Jesus was just sitting there being Jesus, hanging out with Zacchaeus, and loving him. In the middle of lunch, Zacchaeus blurts out, "Behold, Lord, the half of my goods I give to the poor; and if I have taken any thing from any man by false accusation, I restore him fourfold." Luke 19:8, KJV.

He said in essence, "I'm going to repent of the way I've been living." As far as we know, Jesus didn't preach a sermon on covetousness or stealing, but a genuine change came into Zacchaeus' life because of Jesus' love. When you love people, you bring down the walls. As a result, you will have opportunities to share Jesus with those around you.

Once I was flying to India for a mission's trip. I was sitting next to a Hindu woman who had lived in United States with her husband for 11 years. She was flying home to visit her family. As we talked, she asked me what I did for a living, and I told her, "I'm a Christian minister." She said, "Oh." Immediately I sensed a wall went up. After all, she was a Hindu.

I didn't say anything for a while. I just relaxed in my seat. Later, I struck up a conversation. I asked about her family, her children, her husband, and what he did. I was just friendly. I just sincerely cared about her as a fellow human being. I was interested in her life and I told her about my own family. All of a sudden I noticed that the wall was down. Once the wall was down, I said, "Has anyone ever told you about Jesus, and what He did on the cross?"

She said, "No, not really."

Now this woman was in her mid 30's. She had lived in India for 25 years. Then she had moved to the United States, which is supposedly a Christian nation. In the 11 years she lived in the United States, no one had ever told her about Jesus.

"Would it be okay if I shared with you about what Jesus did for you?" I asked. She said, "That would be fine." So I sat on that plane and explained to her about the Gospel of Jesus Christ, how we are all sinners and lost and without hope. I told her about the Fall of our ancestors, Adam and Eve, and how God sent His Son to die for our sins. I told her how He rose from the dead and poured out His Spirit and He will come into our lives if we ask Him. I also explained to her exactly how to receive Jesus Christ as her personal Lord and Savior. At that time she was not ready to receive Christ, but nevertheless the Gospel seed was planted, and I believe that the time will come when the Holy Spirit will bring that conversation back to her remembrance and she will receive Christ as Savior and Lord.

Jesus Teaches Lifestyle Evangelism

"Then said Jesus to them again, Peace be unto you: as my Father hath sent me, even so send I you. And when he had said this, he breathed on them, and saith unto them, Receive ye the Holy Ghost: Whose soever sins ye remit, they are remitted unto them; and whose soever sins ye retain, they are retained." John 20:21-23, KJV.

Here's some real enlightenment concerning lifestyle evangelism. First of all, Jesus said, "Peace be unto you." In Ephesians 6:15, it says we should go forth with the Gospel of peace. You must have peace yourself if you're going to give it to someone else. Lifestyle evangelism is birthed out of your own relationship with God.

"As my Father sent me, even so send I you." You see, we're doing the same thing Jesus did—going forth, helping people, healing people, loving people, and showing them the way to God. Then He breathed on them and said, "Receive ye the Holy Ghost." We need that Holy Spirit power to go and to be effective in reaching people.

Now notice the next amazing statement from the lips of Jesus: "Whose soever sins ye remit, they are remitted unto them; and whose soever sins ye retain, they are retained." Some people have tried to make a doctrine out of this, saying that if you've sinned, you need to go to some special clergy person and confess your sins to them in order to be forgiven. But, I believe that Jesus is giving us a key to successful lifestyle evangelism.

If you are releasing forgiveness, people around you will find forgiveness. If you're exuding judgment, people will find judgment. In many ways, you determine people's future by what you project. The key is your attitude. Jesus was forgiving towards those who had sinned. He never excused sin, but He did forgive sin. For example, the scribes and Pharisees brought a woman to Him who was caught in adultery. They wanted to stone her, but Jesus said, "He that is without sin among you, let him first cast a stone at her." John 8:7, KJV. After they all were convicted of their own sins and left, she stood before Jesus and He said to her, "Neither do I condemn you, go and sin no more. "John 8:11, KJV. He forgave her, and then He charged her to begin living a clean life.

You can't have the attitude, "They deserve judgment." Sure they do, and so do you. It's by the mercy of God that all of us are saved. Certainly, each person must repent individually and find peace with God, but your attitude of love and forgiveness opens the door for them to find mercy. You are God's ambassador. It's up to you to extend His loving, merciful hand to those around you.

Jesus loved people freely. When someone came to Him for healing. He didn't say, "Have you prayed the sinner's prayer? Are you a member of a local church? Do you tithe?" No, He prayed for them and they were healed. He multiplied the fishes and loaves and fed them all, sinners and saints. That's the attitude we need to have. When you do this, people's hearts will open up to you and to the Gospel you proclaim. And not only that, it will release the life of God that is in you to flow out to them.

Expect Miracles in Your Neighborhood

"Verily, verily, I say unto you, He that believeth on me, the works that I do shall he do also; and greater works

than these shall he do; because I go unto my Father." John 14:12, KJV.

Notice this amazing verse is applied to "He that believeth in me." As a believer, you should expect to do the works that Jesus did. Heal the sick. Cast out devils. Raise the dead. That is lifestyle evangelism. Expect miracles, not just in church services, but out in your neighborhood.

I was pastoring a church in a rural area of North Dakota, and our church didn't have a building. We were looking for a piece of land to build on, and there was a farmer who had some land on the edge of town for sale.

I went out to see the land, and the farmer and I got to talking, standing outside, watching the sun go down on the North Dakota prairie. He told me about some sicknesses he had in his body. The compassion of Jesus rose up in me for this man, and I said, "Can I pray for you?" We prayed and he was miraculously healed. His blood work had revealed some real problems in His body. His Triglyceride count was off the charts. But after we prayed, they tested him again and his Triglycerides were normal. The doctor said, "That's not possible." So they tested him two more times. Each time the results came back normal. He was miraculously healed. When you feel the compassion of God within you, that is the Holy Spirit wanting to work through you.

Later on, the doctors discovered a tumor in his colon. I saw him one day at the armory where he worked as a reserve officer. I asked him if I could come to his house and pray with him. As I sat in his living room with him and his wife, we studied the Scriptures together. I laid hands on him in his living room and the glory of the Lord filled that room. I commanded the tumor to shrivel and die, and he immediately felt in his body that he was healed. He had another colonoscopy which revealed that the tumor had shriveled. Before it was the size of a golf ball, but now it was shriveled like a raisin. They removed the tumor, but lost it, so they were not able to do a biopsy. They checked him after he had recovered from the surgery and told him, "You have the colon of an 18-year old." He was completely whole. Jesus is alive and works through the hands of His people. He said these signs shall follow them that believe.

As a believer in Jesus, it is normal that signs would follow you. Let God empower you for signs and wonders. Be filled with the Holy Spirit and expect Him to use you to reach people for Him.

Father, I want to cultivate a lifestyle of evangelism. I want to know You and make You known. Fill me with Your Spirit as I praise and worship You every day of my life. Fill me with Your Word as I read and study and meditate. I want to be an everyday Christian and an everyday witness for You. Every day! Every day! Every day! I believe that I will do the same works that Jesus did.

May my life glorify You Lord, and may You fill the earth with Your glory through me, in Jesus' name. Amen.

Chapter 8

Preaching the Evangelistic Message

"For the preaching of the cross is to them that perish foolishness; but unto us which are saved it is the power of God." 1 Corinthians 1:18, KJV.

In spite of what we have said about sharing one-on-one and lifestyle evangelism, the public proclamation of the Gospel is still a much needed part of the work of evangelism in the earth today. God is emphasizing that every believer is a minister and a witness for Christ, but we still need anointed men and women of God who will stand up and lift their voices to boldly proclaim the glorious Gospel of Christ to the masses of people.

This particular chapter is primarily written to those who publicly proclaim the Gospel, but there are principles here to help any believer with their presentation of the Gospel. Also, it is important for every believer to learn about the ministry of evangelistic proclamation in order to pray and cooperate with the Gospel ministers who are laboring in our midst and on the evangelistic field.

A true evangelistic message expresses the heart of God toward the person who is lost and without hope in this world. It presents the message of the Gospel in the simplest form, so that men and women, boys and girls can respond and give their lives to Jesus Christ.

If someone preaches with a great deal of fire and enthusiasm and is able to stir up a crowd, many will say he or she is evangelistic. But true evangelistic ministry is more about substance than style. Even though a minister's presentation may be rousing and stirring, if he does not clearly present the Gospel message in such a way as it can be understood, received, and acted upon, it is not truly evangelistic.

Many of the fiery messages we hear from gifted ministers are exhortations to the believers, rather than evangelistic messages to reach the lost. Many of the examples that we have of preaching ministry today from the most popular ministers (through their CDs, DVDs, and television programs) are not geared to the lost. These messages are exhortations or teachings for the believers. Therefore, young ministers and those who have a desire to preach evangelistically have little to follow in the way of examples of evangelistic preaching.

If the evangelistic message was proclaimed more clearly from our pulpits, then the members of our congregations would be much more adept at sharing the Gospel with their family and friends. But because the focus is often on everything but the Gospel, many church members are functionally illiterate concerning sharing the Gospel message.

Every Gospel minister, whether he or she is an apostle, prophet, evangelist, pastor, or teacher, should know how to preach evangelistically. Every minister should be following Paul's instruction to "do the work of an evangelist." If there was more training in Bible schools concerning the art and science of preaching the evangelistic message and how to cooperate with the anointing for such a ministry, we would see many more conversions in our churches and in our communities.

Preaching is different from teaching. Preaching is lifting up your voice and proclaiming the Good News. Anointed preaching hits a register on the spirit of man, because it is God's message of deliverance spoken through a vessel that is yielded to Him for that purpose. Teaching is explaining. That's important too, even in the evangelistic message. But preaching accomplishes something on a different realm. It breaks spiritual strongholds. It unlocks the emotions. It brings a conviction. It causes the hearers to rejoice in a God Who saves. We need that kind of preaching today!

I believe that many ministers live and die without ever having learned to preach evangelistically. Some have bought the lie that because they are a pastor or a prophet or a teacher, it is not their job to reach the lost. As a result, many people will spend eternity in hell.

One can not learn everything about preaching evangelistically in a classroom. The greatest training that one can receive is actually getting out there and preaching to the lost. I believe it is difficult for someone to learn how to preach evangelistically by only preaching inside the church house. There are exceptions to this, but normally the local church ministry is orientated toward the believer. The needs of the people in the congregation tend to pull the preacher into subjects such as Christian growth, renewing the mind, family, prayer, and so on. Therefore, the orientation of the minister is inappropriate for developing a proper mind for evangelistic preaching. His thought pattern. as he prepares to preach, is more orientated to building up the people who are already saved.

To develop a proper mind for evangelistic preaching, every minister should look for opportunities to minister to the lost, such as open air services, overseas missions, ministering in jails, prisons, detention centers, nursing homes, and other places where there is a multitude of people who are away from God and need to hear the simple Gospel of Jesus Christ. Then, he or she will begin to learn what it takes to bring a message to someone who does not know Christ.

There are certain basic things that a person must understand to be saved. Sometimes, in our preaching or witnessing, we are talking "Christianeze." We are speaking in a way that the insider (the believer) understands, but the unconverted soul doesn't have a clue. Very often we take for granted that people understand the terms and phrases which we use.

Expressions such as "getting saved," "receiving Jesus," "sin," and "redemption" have little or no relevance in the mind of the unlearned hearers, unless they are explained.

We must go back to Christianity 101 and explain the essential elements of the Gospel in a way that they can understand. For example, we may say that Jesus is the Savior, but this statement has very little relevance unless the person understands what they are being saved from. Therefore they must understand something about judgment, which means they must understand something about sin, which means they must understand something about the Fall, the Creation, and the one true and living God.

When a person makes a decision on insufficient information, it may not produce a true conversion. He may be coming forward or praying a prayer as a result of the charisma of the speaker, an emotional pull, or peer pressure from the group. But, if he understands the Gospel, he can exercise faith in the Savior and make Jesus his Lord, which is what is necessary to obtain salvation.

Let's take a look at some of the basic elements of the evangelistic message.

1. **God made everything good.** There is only one God, who made the sky and stars and sun and the earth and everything that is in it. He made the trees and the grass and the

animals and He made you. When He made everything else, He saw that it was *good*. But when He made people, He saw that it was *very good*. He did not make man to live a miserable life. He did not create us to be ridden with sin, disease, poverty, crime, and social problems. He created us in His own image, with purpose, with dominion, and with dignity.

2. **Man fell into sin and death.** In many cultures around the world, and even in the western society in which we live in today, there is very little consciousness of what sin is, and little fear of God and of His judgment. Therefore, in order to preach evangelistically, we must lay the ground work for an understanding of the Fall of man. Through Adam, sin and death were passed on to the human race, along with the resulting curses and eternal judgment. As these things are preached, the Holy Spirit can then use them to bring conviction to the heart of the hearer and a revelation of the need in their life for change.

3. **Jesus Christ came to save you.** It should seem obvious to us, but sometimes we try to get people to respond to the Gospel without first presenting God's answer to man's dilemma, Christ and Him crucified. Once Billy Graham had preached his heart out trying to win the lost, but his message fell flat and produced little results. Later, a business man pointed

out to him that he had failed to present the cross of Jesus Christ as the answer. Once we have presented the problem (man's dilemma and the impending judgment), then we must present the people with the only way out, Jesus Christ.

We can do this by sharing a brief overview of the life of Christ—His virgin birth, His sinless life, His teaching, His miracles, His death at Calvary as a substitution for our sins, and His resurrection. Of course this makes for wonderful preaching, which has the power to inspire the believers that are in attendance as well as to capture the heart of the unbeliever. This is the opportunity to present the love and mercy and goodness of God, Who sent His son to die for our sins. This also begins to really release the power of the Holy Spirit to draw the people to Jesus.

4. **You must receive Christ.** When you present Jesus as Savior, it is good to point out that He is the Savior of the whole world. No one is left out of the mercy-plan of God. But then we must declare the absolute necessity of personally receiving the gift of eternal life. The message must become personal to that individual.

It is good to press home the point that God is looking for a response now, that He is the one who has sent you as His ambassador with His message of love, and that He is wants to know their response. Scriptures such as John 1:12 can be used effectively, "But as many as received him, to them gave he power to become the sons of God, even to them that believe on his name:" John 1:12, KJV.

Tell them about the supernatural element of the salvation experience—about the power of God to change a heart and that they can receive a new birth and a new life in Christ. They should be made to understand that God will forgive all their sins and give them a gift of righteousness through Jesus Christ and will give them a desire and the ability to live for Him.

Then they should be clearly instructed on how to make this decision. Two things are essential at that point. They must *repent* and *believe* the Gospel. "Now after that John was put in prison, Jesus came into Galilee, preaching the gospel of the kingdom of God, And saying, The time is fulfilled, and the kingdom of God is at hand: repent ye, and believe the gospel." Mark 1:14, 15, KJV.

Repent. The word repentance is another term that must be clearly understood. They must understand that they are making a life-altering decision to turn away from sin and to follow Jesus as Lord. It means to change your mind and change your ways. Illustrations or personal testimony can be used to drive home this point. If the people have been idol worshippers, tell them that when they receive Jesus they should throw all the idols out of their lives and homes. It must also be emphasized that this is a change of heart, that they are not saved by their works. However, they must have a change of direction from sin to God.

Believe the Gospel. This is a wonderful opportunity to reinforce the power of the Gospel through faith in the cross. By believing in what God has done for them in Christ, they receive the benefit of the Gospel, eternal life.

Helpful Hints for Gospel Preaching

God can use whatever knowledge you have to reach people for Christ, but a strong biblical foundation is a great help to the evangelistic preacher. It is helpful to have a grasp of the story of the Bible and have a clear comprehension of the redemption that is in Christ. These things must be real and personal in the heart of the preacher. Also, it is helpful to have God's Word embedded in your heart through meditation, so that you can draw out scriptures at will from within your heart to use during your message. You can use key scriptures, such as those in Romans (chapters 1-5) concerning salvation, and the Gospel of John (especially chapters 1, 3 & 14), and the first three chapters of the book of Genesis. Also, key predictive scriptures from Isaiah and other prophets concerning Christ are helpful, such as Isaiah 53. Although you are preaching the simple basics of the faith, it is important for the evangelistic preacher to have a strong doctrinal foundation and a good grasp of the Word of God to build his message upon.

Once you establish these foundations firmly in your mind and heart, along with having appropriate scriptures in your heart as arrows ready to fly, you can flow with the direction of the Holy Spirit and find great freedom in your preaching. The Holy Spirit can then emphasize certain truths or elements of the message as needed for the particular audience.

Before you preach to an audience that does not know you, tell them something about yourself. Speak warmly and sincerely, so that they can relate to you as a person. If they first open their heart to the messenger, it will help them to receive the message.

Speak directly from your heart as a compassionate friend to your hearers. Find a scripture text to use as a basis for your message. Read that in the beginning and then preach from your heart. A 20-minute message from your heart is better than an hour of stiff, uninspired reading of notes from a page. Start where you are and rise up in the glory of God. Then call the people to repentance at the foot of the cross.

I once heard the story that taught me a lot about the kind of attitude it takes to be an effective

Gospel preacher. Someone had told Billy Graham about a young man who had been doing research and studying the subject of evangelism at Wheaton College. Mr. Graham then asked, "Do you think he would be willing to sit down and talk with me to help me improve my Gospel presentation?" Here was the man that many say is the greatest evangelist in the world, and he was looking for help with his Gospel presentation. What about the rest of us?

We need to continually sharpen our arrows and develop the skills necessary to be effective soul winners. We are carrying the only message that can save men's eternal souls. May God help us to be effective in bringing forth that message to a spiritually destitute world.

Help me Father, to hide the Word of Your salvation in my heart, that I might give a clear presentation of the Gospel to those who need it. Help me to proclaim Your Gospel clearly and fearlessly, in Jesus' name. Amen.

Chapter 9

The Ministry of the Evangelist

"Then Philip went down to the city of Samaria, and preached Christ unto them." Acts 8:5, KJV.

For many people, an evangelist is someone who preaches on television and wears a white suit. For others, the image in their mind is someone with a bouffant haircut and a travel trailer. Leaders of a large Pentecostal denomination were asked about the meaning of the term "evangelist," and they stated that an evangelist is anyone who travels around from church to church and preaches and teaches.

The term "televangelist" has become part of the common vernacular in our times and is used for anyone who uses the medium of television to preach or teach or raise money. In fact, many people have the impression that evangelists are some kind of charlatan with their hand in people's pockets.

But in fact, most evangelists are just simple men and women of God with a calling to proclaim the Good News of Jesus Christ and to see people receive forgiveness, freedom from sin, and peace with God. The Bible word translated evangelist means "a messenger of good." It comes from a root word meaning "to proclaim glad tidings."

The evangelist is one of five different types of ministers who are described in Paul's letter to the church at Ephesus: "And he gave some, apostles; and some, prophets; and some, evangelists; and some, pastors and teachers; For the perfecting of the saints, for the work of the ministry, for the edifying of the body of Christ:" Ephesians 4:11, 12, KJV.

These ministers (apostles, prophets, evangelists, pastors, and teachers) are supernaturally endowed and anointed gifts to the Church, who are called to help bring Christ's Church to maturity and fulfillment. In order for the Church to fulfill her destiny in this world, we need a restoration of all these gifts to the Church. None of these gifts have passed away. They will all be in operation and functioning until we all come to the fulness of Christ. These gifts are given to the Church "Till we all come in the unity of the faith, and of the knowledge of the Son of God, unto a perfect man, unto the measure of the stature of the fulness of Christ:" Ephesians 4:13, KJV. The last time I checked, we have not arrived to the fulness of Christ, so these gifts (all of them) are still much needed in the Church today.

Let's take a quick look at these five ministries and then we will focus more specifically on the ministry of the evangelist.

1. The apostle is a "sent one." He is sent by God on a mission to invade society, plant churches, and establish the will of God in a particular area. Many missionaries are apostles. In

fact, the root of both words (missionary and apostle) is "to send." Apostle comes from a Greek word. Missionary comes from a Latin word.

2. The prophet is especially gifted in revelation gifts and is concerned with purity and divine purpose in the Church.

3. The evangelist is a proclaimer of the Good News. The evangelist has a ministry to the world and to the Church and is charged with inspiring and encouraging Christ's Body, the Church, to evangelize the world.

4. The pastor is a shepherd of the sheep. He is concerned with teaching and watching over members of the Body of Christ.

5. The teacher is an instructor in biblical truth. All pastors are teachers, but not all teachers are pastors. Some teachers are traveling ministers. Others have the focus of their ministries on teaching and training in Bible colleges or holding seminars.

These five ministry gifts are all ministers of the Gospel. Each ministers in the Word of God and each has a role in "the perfecting of the saints for the work of the ministry." The pastor is only one of five different ministry gifts given by God to the Church, and all five gifts are necessary for God's work to ever be accomplished in the earth.

Not everyone in Christ's Body is called to one of these fivefold ministry gifts, and yet each member of the Christ's Body does have a ministry. It may be to serve the church in the nursery, children's department, or as an usher or greeter. It may be to pray or to give. And all of us are called to be witnesses for Christ in our daily life. Sometimes people have the idea that the only way they can serve God is in a pulpit ministry, but in reality the best way that each of us can serve God is to find our God-directed place of service and to be faithful in it.

Now, all of these five gifts are ministers of the Word. You might find any of them ministering the Word of God from the pulpit. They all, from time to time, preach or teach, pray for people's needs, and in general minister (or serve) people spiritually. In many ways they are similar.

The difference comes in the focus or emphasis of their ministry. The focus of the apostle is the establishment of the Church in the nations and territories of the world. The focus of the prophet is to look into the Spirit and bring supernatural revelation and purity to the Church. The focus of the evangelist is to proclaim the Gospel and win souls. The focus of the pastor is the care for the flock. The focus of the teacher is to instruct the Church and to establish the people in pure doctrine.

Each minister should seek to operate in his or her specific calling or emphasis. What we all should do, however, is to be mindful of the great cause of the Lord in all of our ministries. This is why the Apostle Paul told Timothy, who was a pastor, to "do the work of an evangelist." (2 Tim. 4:5)

Some ministers are able to get more people saved by accident than others do on purpose. The teacher, for example, may function most effectively in his office, focusing on instructing the saints in the the pure Word of God. Then, he gives an invitation for the lost to come to Christ and they come. Why? Because he's functioning in his anointing and at the same time being mindful of the lost. Each gift is needed. That's why the Lord anoints people for a specific purpose. But ultimately, the goal is to reach this world for Jesus Christ.

I have a friend who has a ministry helping people to be more effective in the workplace, to see their job as a calling, and do it with dignity and honor. This opens opportunities for him to minister to people with many differing spiritual backgrounds, from atheists to born again Christians, and everything in between. Many people are getting saved as a result of His seminars. So, I encourage you to function in your anointing and the place of your calling, but to be mindful of the lost.

We see an example of this in the ministry of the Apostle Paul, "And I, brethren, when I came to you, came not with excellency of speech or of wisdom, declaring unto you the testimony of God. For I determined not to know any thing among you, save Jesus Christ, and him crucified. And I was with you in weakness, and in fear, and in much trembling. And my speech and my preaching was not with enticing words of man's wisdom, but in demonstration of the Spirit and of power: That your faith should not stand in the wisdom of men, but in the power of God." 1 Corinthians 2:1-5, KJV.

Here, Paul, in his letter to the church at Corinth, remembers when he first came to them and ministered the Word of God. He states that at that time, when they were unknowledgeable in the things of God, as he ministered to them, he "determined not to know any thing among you, but Jesus Christ and Him crucified." In other words, he made up his mind to preach the simple Gospel. Paul knew other things. He was quite capable of ministering on many different subjects, but he knew that the one thing they needed was the simple Gospel of Christ, so that they could be born again. Then and only then could they move on to the deeper truths.

Paul's focus as an apostle was expanding the kingdom of God and establishing the Church of Jesus Christ. But before he could establish the church in Corinth, he had to "do the work of an evangelist." He had to win some souls. He went on to say that among them that are mature, he spoke "the wisdom of God in a mystery, even the hidden wisdom...the deep things of God." (1 Cor. 2:7,10, partial) But in order to minister to unsaved people, he "determined" to proclaim the simple truth of a Savior who died for our sins on Calvary. Every minister should make it his or her business to win souls to Christ, not just the evangelist. Nowhere in the Scriptures is Paul called an evangelist, although he did call himself a preacher (proclaimer). He was called as an apostle, but part of that ministry, like it should be in all of our ministries, was soul winning.

Now to the Evangelist

"Then Philip went down to the city of Samaria, and preached Christ unto them." Acts 8:5, KJV.

Now, let's look more closely at the ministry of the evangelist. The message of the evangelist is "Christ and Him crucified." It's the message of the Messiah, the Savior of the world. It's the message that "God so loved the world that He gave His only begotten son…" This is the predominant message of the evangelist. This is where his ministry functions most effectively.

An evangelist is a specialist. This is his special area of gifting—proclaiming the Good News. It doesn't mean that other ministers cannot or should not preach the simple Gospel. On the contrary, they should. In fact, none of us should ever stray too far from the simple Gospel. It is the foundation of everything we do. But for the evangelist, it's his heart and soul. He lives to preach the Good News.

Notice the results of Philip's preaching: "And the people with one accord gave heed unto those things which Philip spake, hearing and seeing the miracles which he did. For unclean spirits, crying with loud voice, came out of many that were possessed with them: and many taken with palsies, and that were lame, were healed. And there was great joy in that city." Acts 8:6-8, KJV.

The Good News brings great joy! As the Scripture says, "How beautiful are the feet of them that preach the Gospel of peace, and brings glad tidings of good things!" If you're an evangelist, somebody's going to be glad to see you coming their way, because you're going to give them some good news about their eternal destiny. You're going to let them know that there is a God who loves them and forgives them and heals them. Oh, happy days! The evangelist is coming to town!

Even church people need this type of ministry. Sometimes God's people have been taught and taught and discipled and told how to live the Christian life, but they just need somebody to come and preach the happy Good News. There's just something refreshing about hearing it again, basking in the truth, and remembering once again all the benefits of the Gospel. In fact, as we pointed out earlier, all five ministry gifts are given "for the perfecting of the saints, for the work of the ministry, for the building of the Body of Christ." So, the evangelist's gift is needed inside the church as well as outside the church. The job of the evangelist is to inspire, encourage, train, and model evangelism, so that the entire Body of Christ may come into the proper alignment for reaching the lost of this world.

Notice when Philip came down to Samaria, the people listened to him "hearing and seeing the miracles which he did." The Scriptures tell us that God confirms His word with signs following. As we go forth, preaching the Good News of the resurrected Savior, He will work with us, demonstrating that Jesus is alive. These miracles are part of the divine equipment of the evangelist, which help him to reach the unreachable and to touch the untouchable.

After Philip held his campaign in Samaria, the apostles from Jerusalem came to minister further to the people: "Now when the apostles which were at Jerusalem heard that Samaria had received the word of God, they sent unto them Peter and John: Who, when they were come down, prayed for them, that they might receive the Holy Ghost: (For as yet he was fallen upon none of them: only they were baptized in the name of the Lord Jesus.) Then laid they their hands on them, and they received the Holy Ghost." Acts 8:14-17, KJV.

So Philip had preached the Gospel of Christ. He had done miracles and cast out devils. He had baptized many converts, yet the apostles came down and ministered to the people so that they might receive the baptism of the Holy Spirit.

So, Philip was apparently not especially gifted on teaching on the baptism of the Holy Spirit or for praying for people to receive the baptism of the Holy Spirit. He was no doubt baptized in the Holy Spirit himself, as evidenced by the signs and wonders in his ministry, but evidently he was not especially gifted in ministering the baptism of the Holy Spirit to others.

Now, we could be in danger of painting ourselves into a corner here by stating that evangelists are gifted in healing the sick, but not ministering the baptism of the Holy Spirit. However, we know many evangelists are used greatly in helping people to receive this precious gift. It would probably be more appropriate for us to draw the following truth from the biblical account: not all ministers are gifted to do all things. Therefore we need one another. We need to take a team approach to ministry, rather than operating as a one-man show.

Philip had a tremendous Gospel crusade in Samaria and many came to Christ. He could have stayed there and enjoyed all the accolades and the fruit of his labors. But the Lord had other plans: "And the angel of the Lord spake unto Philip, saying, Arise, and go toward the south unto the way that goeth down from Jerusalem unto Gaza, which is desert. And he arose and went: and, behold, a man of Ethiopia, an eunuch of great authority under Candace queen of the Ethiopians, who had the charge of all her treasure, and had come to Jerusalem for to worship, Was returning, and sitting in his chariot read Esaias the prophet." Acts 8:26-28, KJV.

So this evangelist left this tremendous meeting and the crowds of people coming to Christ in order to minister to one man, the Ethiopian eunuch. Now, again, we need to be careful not to draw absolute conclusions from one example, but the evangelist is often "on the go." He is sent to bring the Gospel to those who need it and to reap the harvest wherever it is ripe. Most often, it is not a stationary ministry, like the pastor. The evangelist is on assignment by the Lord. And whether he is preaching to a multitude or one eunuch, he is on a mission to take the Gospel to the world. (By the way, in this book, I am using the pronoun "he" editorially. Thank God, there are female evangelists as well!)

Now let's look at Philip's encounter with the Ethiopian eunuch: "Then the Spirit said unto Philip, Go near, and join thyself to this chariot. And Philip ran thither to him, and heard him read the prophet Esaias, and said, Understandest thou what thou readest? And he said, How can I, except some man should guide me? And he desired Philip that he would come up and sit with him. The place of the scripture which he read was this, He was led as a sheep to the slaughter; and like a lamb dumb before his shearer, so opened he not his mouth: In his humiliation his judgment was taken away: and who shall declare his generation? for his life is taken from the earth. And the eunuch answered Philip, and said, I pray thee, of whom speaketh the prophet this? of himself, or of some other man? Then Philip opened his mouth, and began at the same scripture, and preached unto him Jesus." Acts 8:29-35, KJV.

Here again we see that Philip's message was Jesus. The eunuch was reading in Isaiah and Philip began at that same scripture and preached Jesus. No matter where he starts, an evangelist always gets back to his main message, Jesus Christ and His crucifixion.

This Is the Hour of the Evangelist

Though very few realize it, this is the hour of the evangelist. As we look at the Church, there are very few ministers functioning in the office of the evangelist. The Church as a whole seems to have little interest in this gift. But now is the time to embrace the evangelistic gift. This is the gift most closely aligned with the Great Commission, and it must be embraced in this hour in order to see the fulfillment of the move of God in the earth in these last days. It must be emphasized. It must be used. God's purposes will not be accomplished without all of the ministry gifts in operation.

In recent years, we've seen a restoration of the ministries of the apostles and the prophets. But for the picture to be complete, we must also see a restoration of true God-called evangelists. Each gift has its part to fulfill in the culmination of history. There must be a restoration of *all* the fivefold ministry gifts and an impartation of these gifts to the Body of Christ before the Lord returns. We should cultivate the development of all the ministry gifts in our churches and Bible schools, including the gift of the evangelist. If someone has the burning desire to reach to the lost and to serve as an evangelist, that desire should be encouraged and cultivated.

The Evangelist and the Local Church

Some have thought that the evangelist's ministry, since he is given to the cause of reaching the lost, should not have any connection with local churches, but that he should spend all his time and energy in the highways and byways reaching the lost. However, according to Ephesians 4, the evangelist is one of five gifts given for bringing the Body of Christ to maturity. To be effective, every ministry gift must have a connection to the visible Church of Jesus Christ. The evangelist must work together with local churches to bring in and preserve the harvest and to train and inspire God's people to do the work of evangelism.

The evangelist has an anointing to impart to the Body of Christ. The passion, the gifting, and the message of the evangelist must be released to the Church, so that the Church can fulfill its mission and accomplish its destiny. The impartation of the evangelist, like the impartation of all the five-fold ministry gifts, is necessary for the perfecting of the saints for the work of the ministry and the building up of the Body of Christ.

When the evangelist comes to town, it's harvest time. It's time to pull out all the stops and do all you can to bring in the lost. The evangelist has a message that the friends, neighbors, and relatives of church members need to hear. The body of believers must be activated to reach out to those around them and to invite them. Every effort should be made to promote the meetings and reach out to the community. When an evangelist is coming to town, the believers should be on their faces crying out for lost souls. They should be inviting everyone they can to come and hear the Good News. Unnecessary activities should be canceled and every department and every person in the church should be focused on evangelism. It's time to team up with the evangelist to reach the community for Christ.

Utilize the evangelist to preach the Gospel message outside of the church walls. While he is in your town, take him to the nursing home, jails, detention centers, anywhere there is a crowd to listen to the message. When possible, organize crusades with the other churches in the community. Make it a united community-wide effort to reach the lost and bring home those that are away from God.

The ministry of the evangelist can help bring revival in the church. The themes most often preached by the evangelist, concerning redemption, faith, repentance, restoration, and healing, are much needed in the church world today. Many discouraged saints could use a good shot in the arm of Gospel medicine. This ministry can augment the work of the local pastor in a precious and powerful way, and can cause an excitement about the Lord to spill over into the world around us. There's something about bringing in a God-anointed evangelist that will bring life and zeal to the congregation. It is God's intention that the various ministry gifts complement one another in order to accomplish the will of God in the earth.

Here are some of the ways that a local church and an evangelist work together to fulfill the Great Commission:

The church can hold evangelistic meetings. Most meetings in the local church are geared primarily for the edification of the believer. A local church can bring the evangelist in to hold special meetings with the purpose of reaching the lost and helping people to be restored to fellowship with the Lord. It can be a church crusade, held at the normal place the church meets, or it can be held at a neutral location, or it can be a cooperative effort with a group of churches in a specific area. Local churches can also sponsor special outreaches in nearby communities where the church is desiring to establish a satellite or daughter church. Special services can also be held in jails, prisons, and nursing homes. Through prayer and by seeking God for creative ideas, the local church and the evangelist can work together to touch lives and build the church of Jesus Christ.

The evangelist can inspire and encourage the congregation. By sharing testimonies, missions reports, and by sharing his burden for the lost, the evangelist can encourage people to get involved in God's great plan to reach the world. The evangelist, as he shares about his experiences in winning souls, miracles, and changed lives, can renew a sense of respect and urgency for God's number one job, evangelism.

The evangelist can train the congregation. The evangelist can hold classes and seminars to teach what he has learned from the Bible and his own experience about proclaiming the Gospel, being a witness, and reaching the people with the Gospel. Very often, the Lord gives the evangelist a desire to multiply his ministry by training others. For example, Billy Graham has used a "Christian Life and Witness" course in conjunction which his crusades. Some have said that there has been greater fruit from these classes than from the actual crusades.

The local church can also unite with the evangelist in giving and receiving. As part of their missions vision, the local church can support the ongoing work of evangelism through prayers, finances, friendship, and mutual encouragement. By sowing seeds from the heart for the ongoing work of evangelism, the local church can expect to reap fruit that will remain and continue to multiply. This is helpful to the evangelist, because through the partnership of churches and individuals, he is able to focus on reaching needy people, without concern about offerings to support his ministry. Many churches have caught the vision that a traveling evangelist is worthy of missionary support.

The ministry of the evangelist will be restored to full function once again in the Church in these end days. Jesus said, "And this gospel of the kingdom shall be preached in all the world for a witness unto all nations; and then shall the end come." Matthew 24:14, KJV. The ministry of the evangelist will figure prominently in the fulfillment of that prophecy, both through his ministry of directly reaching the lost and by influencing and training others to share the Good News. The Lord is igniting all of us with a passion to reach those who do not know Him.

Dear Father, I thank You for the gift of the evangelist and all the ministry gifts that You have given to Your Church. Help me to cooperate with Your plan for developing Your Church into mature, strong, faithful witnesses with the help of the ministry gifts. Help me to work together with Your evangelists to reach this world for Jesus Christ, in Jesus' name. Amen.

Chapter 10

Put Your Money Where Your Mouth Is

"For where your treasure is, there will your heart be also." (Matthew 6:21, KJV).

If you want to find out what is really important to a person or a family or a business or an organization, you can do so by looking at their spending patterns.

For example, if someone spends $2,500 a month on playing golf, it would be very obvious that golf is a major priority in their life. If 30 percent of a person's budget is used for retirement savings, then you could easily see that financial security is a huge priority.

Similarly, in the business world, we can see a demonstration of the heart and purpose of a company by what they spend their money on. For example, if a huge percentage of a company's budget is spent on advertising, then you could readily see that image is a huge priority for that company. Our hearts are revealed, perhaps most clearly, by where we spend our money.

Once I was talking to the Lord about tithing to my local church. The Spirit of God spoke up within me and said these words, "Put your money where your mouth is." I instantly knew what I was supposed to do. With all my heart, I believe in the local church. I believe that it is the heart of God's work and His plan in the earth. When I minister to people, I tell them, "Get involved in a local church that preaches the Bible." So, I knew what the Lord meant when He said, "Put your money where your mouth is." My tithe belongs in the local church.

Likewise, many of us say that evangelism is important. Perhaps, we deeply believe that reaching the lost is God's number one job. However, our giving does not always reflect that conviction. God says, "Put your money where your mouth is." If you believe in evangelism, invest in evangelism!

The same goes for local churches. The churches should invest in missions, both here and abroad, and their missions giving should be weighted toward giving for the cause of evangelism and discipleship, rather than giving all their money to meeting natural physical needs. If Jesus left us a Great Commission that says, "Go into all the world and preach the Gospel," we should not spend all our resources in meeting the material needs of people. Yes, meet the needs, but also give them the Gospel, which has the power to change their lives, both in this world and throughout eternity.

The overall priority of the church in America is not as it should be, in terms of reaching the unreached and telling the untold the message of salvation through Jesus Christ. Much of the money spent on world missions, for example, goes to nations that are already largely evangelized. According to the World Evangelization Research Center, 91% of all Christian outreach and evangelism does not target non-Christians, but targets other Christians in previously evangelized countries, cities, peoples, populations, or situations. Not that these places don't need continued ministry, but when you consider that the nations that are largely unevangelized are severely neglected, it's time to seriously reprioritize our giving. Oswald Chambers said, "So long as there is a human being who does not know Jesus Christ, I am his debtor to serve him until he does."

Jesus spoke about the shepherd who left the 99 and went after the one lost sheep. "What man of you, having an hundred sheep, if he lose one of them, doth not leave the ninety and nine in the wilderness, and go after that which is lost, until he find it? And when he hath found it, he layeth it on his shoulders, rejoicing. And when he cometh home, he calleth together his friends and neighbours, saying unto them, Rejoice with me; for I have found my sheep which was lost. I say unto you, that likewise joy shall be in heaven over one sinner that repenteth, more than over ninety and nine just persons, which need no repentance." Luke 15:4-7, KJV.

Heaven rejoices over one sinner who repents more than 99 people who need no repentance, but too often we put all our resources into caring for the 99 and very little into reaching the lost sheep. If evangelism is God's number one job, then each of us individually, regardless of our financial status or income level, must look inside to see where our treasure is. Does our giving really reflect a heart for souls? Are we being biblical and Spirit-led in our giving and in the management of the resources which God has given us?

We Need to Hold the Ropes

"For whosoever shall call upon the name of the Lord shall be saved. How then shall they call on him in whom they have not believed? and how shall they believe in him of whom they have not heard? and how shall they hear without a preacher? And how shall they preach, except they be sent? as it is written, How beautiful are the feet of them that preach the gospel of peace, and bring glad tidings of good things!" Romans 10:13-15, KJV.

Missionaries and evangelists, in particular, must be sent. The Church (God's people) must send them into the harvest fields. In most cases, the resources for their ministries will not be supplied by the people they are ministering to. God's people must undertake to support the work which God has ordained in the harvest fields. This is part of the privilege that each of us has in cooperating with the Lord of the harvest.

When William Carey, the founder of the modern missionary movement, was about to move as a missionary to India to spread the Gospel, he spoke to the missionary society which was sending him. He said he was going deep, deep into a mine shaft to mine for precious souls. "I will go down the mine, if you will all hold the ropes for me."

Financial support, prayers, and encouragement are all essential ingredients for Gospel workers. Whether ministers are sent forth from a prosperous nation or from a place that is less prosperous, those that remain back home should do all that they can to support those that are going down into the mine for precious souls. Giving to Gospel-preaching ministries is the great privilege of all believers, and it yields eternal rewards.

You Have Power to Make a Difference

A sports article stated that an NBA star was "disappointed" with his 85 million dollar contract. I wonder, how can you be disappointed with 85 million dollars? I can't help but thinking about what we could do with just one of those million dollars. How many souls could we reach? How many churches could we build? How many missionaries could we help?

Now, most of us don't have 85 million dollar basketball contracts, but the truth is that God can use what we do have to do great and mighty things. What can we do? Here are some thoughts:

Use what you've got. God's Word says that He gives seed to the sower. God has placed some seeds in your life. I once heard a testimony about someone who started out giving shirt buttons in the offering plate. Now he is giving multiplied thousands to missions and evangelism. Don't be consumed with what you *don't* have. Use what you *do* have and ask God to multiply it that you may have more to give.

Seek God carefully as to where you should give. Sadly, not all the money that is given to "Christian" causes ends up in the right places. Some ends up in the hands of unscrupulous people. And some goes to causes which do not truly further the Gospel. It's great to help people in need, but the most important need is that people would receive eternal life. Seek to support the work of the Gospel in under-evangelized nations and places. Support ministries that are using the resources they have to proclaim the Gospel in your nation and around the world. If they are a mercy ministry or a relief agency, make sure that they are not only feeding people's bellies, but also their souls. Let's adjust our giving in such a way as to bring the greatest impact for the Kingdom of God. We should support ministries which are doing real Kingdom business in a God-honoring way. Let's get the most bang for our buck.

Pray for a transfer of wealth. The Bible says, "A good man leaveth an inheritance to his children's children: and the wealth of the sinner is laid up for the just." Proverbs 13:22, KJV. Let's pray and believe for a transfer of wealth from the kingdom of darkness into the Kingdom of light. In reality, there is no lack of money. Let's pray that the money that is being wasted on trivial pursuits would find its way into the hands of God's people, so they could use it to reach the lost. And let's pray that God's people, as they prosper, would not get caught up in the cares of the world and the deceitfulness of riches, but would use what God gives them to further the Kingdom of God.

Attend a local church that is reaching the lost and hurting. Many Christians give the greatest share of their contributions to their local church. That's good, if that particular church is supporting evangelism and missions and reaching out to the world around them. But if the local church is all about just serving and conserving the local congregation, you are wasting your time and money there. Get involved in something that's making a difference in the world. Find a church that's preaching the Good News, encouraging people to be born again, making disciples, and reaching out to a lost and dying world. The value of a local church is determined not by its seating capacity, but it's sending capacity.

Give of yourself to prayer. Don't think that because your financial resources are limited, you have nothing to give. Your prayers avail much. Study the Scriptures. Learn your authority in prayer over the forces of darkness. Be a part of God's mighty army who give themselves in prayer for the cause of world evangelism. God says, "Ask of me, and I shall give thee the heathen for thine inheritance, and the uttermost parts of the earth for thy possession." Psalms 2:8, KJV. The Apostle Paul was continually asking for prayer. Evangelists and missionaries need prayer support to accomplish their mission. Pray for a spirit of encouragement, boldness, and anointing to preach the Word. Pray for open doors and for the resources they need. Pray for their spouses, their children, their natural life, their emotions, and their health. It's all part of "holding the ropes."

There are many fine missionaries and evangelists who need your prayers, financial support, and encouragement. Ask God to show you who He wants you to support with your prayer and finances. Give yourself to prayer and you will see eternal results. Remember, your voice counts in the Kingdom of God. As we all pull together and hear and obey the voice of the Lord, we will prevail against the Kingdom of darkness.

Dear Father, thank You for Your provision in my life. You give seed to the sower and bread to the eater, so I thank You that I do have seed to sow. As I sow my seed into Your Gospel ministry, it will multiply and produce a harvest, in my life and in the world. Thank You, Father, my treasure is in You and Your eternal Kingdom, in Jesus name. Amen.

Chapter 11

Let's Unite to Reach the World

"Behold, how good and how pleasant it is for brethren to dwell together in unity! It is like the precious ointment upon the head, that ran down upon the beard, even Aaron's beard: that went down to the skirts of his garments; As the dew of Hermon, and as the dew that descended upon the mountains of Zion: for there the LORD commanded the blessing, even life for evermore."
Psalms 133:1-3, KJV.

The 133rd Psalm is actually a worship song about unity. It is "good and pleasant," the Scripture says, "for the brethren to dwell together in unity." The song speaks of "precious ointment," emblematic of the anointing of the Holy Spirit and God's blessings that come as a result of such unity. It was written at the time when all of Israel came together under King David's leadership after a long time of separation and division. This was a great period of rejoicing, excitement, and victory over the oneness of God's people.

This anointing and blessing are sorely missing in the church world today. All too often, instead of unity and love, we have strife, division, and confusion, and as a result we are missing much of what the Lord has for us. We may be individually anointed, but we are falling short of the level of power and blessing which we could have if we would learn to flow together in a corporate anointing.

I believe when we are captivated by the Lord's vision for reaching the world, many of our divisions and struggles will melt away. When we see what the Lord's real passion is, and how He has invited us to come away with Him and to work in the vineyard, we will see a progression in the Church that we have never seen before. I'm talking about a real revival—a revival of righteousness and a unity birthed by the Spirit that will make our separatist doctrines seem meaningless.

When Solomon's temple was dedicated, the Bible says that the Levites "were as one, to make one sound to be heard in praising and thanking the Lord." Together they said, "For He is good, and His mercy endures forever." As a result of their harmonious worship, the Bible says that a cloud of glory filled the temple so that the priests could no longer stand up, because of the power and presence of the Lord. (2 Chronicles 5:11-14)

Likewise, we see on the day of Pentecost, that the believers were "with one accord in one place" and suddenly the Holy Spirit came and filled them all. (Acts 2:1-4) Three thousand people got saved that day. Such is the power and presence of God when we come together in unity.

The corporate anointing can accomplish much more than the individual anointing. And in fact, the anointing upon an individual can easily be dissipated by disunity and lack of harmony in the group. This is true in our individual churches and also in the Body of Christ at large.

In this wonderful song written by David, we read, "It is like the precious ointment upon the head, that ran down upon the beard, even Aaron's beard: that went down to the skirts of his garments..." Now, I don't know about you, but when I read the Old Testament, I read it with New Testament eyes. I realize it was originally written for natural Israel, but it was inspired by the Holy Spirit with the mind of Christ, and the Lord really looks at us (the Church) as the Commonwealth of Israel. We have been grafted in, and we are spiritual Jews, according to the Scriptures. (See Ephesians 2:12 and Romans 2:29.)

Now, we know that the head of the Body is the Lord Jesus Christ. The ointment that flows from the head is the anointing of the Holy Spirit that issues forth from the head of the Church, Jesus. This is the world's greatest anointing, because the Scriptures tell us that God has anointed Jesus "with the oil of gladness above thy fellows." (Ps. 47:5) When we are flowing in the "Jesus anointing," we will rejoice and be glad, and see many miracles to glorify the Son.

The Scripture says that this anointing flows down upon Aaron's beard. The beard represents maturity. Maturity is required to carry the anointing and to allow it to function in the earth. Aaron was the high priest under the Old Testament. For us as New Testament believers, this speaks of the anointing of our high priest, Jesus. This anointing is now upon the ministry gifts and the Body of Christ. This "high priest" anointing is designed to flow down to the skirts of His garment, that is, throughout the whole Body, in order to touch the world.

As a result of this anointing, there is blessing! God's presence brings blessing to the Church and to the world. The dew of Hermon and the dew upon Mt. Zion are symbolic of this blessing, flowing forth and bringing refreshing. Both Hermon and Zion are mountains which receive a dousing of dew, even in dry seasons. The dew speaks of refreshing and a moistening of the hearts and watering of the things of God.

Mt. Zion is emblematic of the Church. It was the high place in the city of the King, Jerusalem. Hermon was also considered a sacred place, which is located in the north of Palestine and is visible from Lebanon, Syria, and Jordan. The dew on Hermon represents the blessing of God that comes on all nations and people through the unity of the believers.

This place of unity is where the Lord commanded the blessing, even life forevermore. In other words, when the brethren dwell together in unity, there will be a corporate anointing, and as a result, there will be blessing in the Church and people will get saved. People getting saved is the mission of the Church. That's why we are here on the earth. It is the thing that is most important to the Lord. So, if we walk in unity with the brethren, we contribute to people getting saved. If we are not walking in harmony, we are contributing to their destruction.

Our Unity Will Touch the World

Jesus also told us that the unity of His Church would touch the world. In the 17th chapter of the Gospel of John, He prayed to the Father, "That they all may be one; as thou, Father, art in me, and I in thee, that they also may be one in us: that the world may believe that thou hast sent me." John 17:21, KJV. Jesus also says, "By this shall all men know that ye are my disciples, if ye have love one to another." John 13:35, KJV.

I was attracted to the Lord because of the love I saw in His people, both a love for Him and a love for one another. True Christian love is our greatest commodity and our greatest soul winning tool. If the Church at large could flow in God's love, our local churches would be full and the world would be won to Jesus. It should be our great quest in life to walk in love.

How many of us have visited a local church, whether on vacation or while searching for a place to fellowship, only to find the congregation turned inward or with strife in the air, and colder than a dead fish? Imagine what it is like for an unbeliever to visit such a place. Many walk away from such places, vowing never to visit another church. How sad it is to squander such wonderful opportunities because of callous indifference to the needs of others.

Don't Miss Your Divine Connections

"After these things the Lord appointed other seventy also, and sent them two and two before his face into every city and place, whither he himself would come." Luke 10:1, KJV.

When Jesus sent out His disciples, He sent them two and two. He knew that they would need one another as they reached out to a lost, dying, sighing, crying humanity. They would require support, encouragement, and prayer in order to accomplish their mission. They would need someone on their team.

When Jesus sent out these teams of two, I have to imagine that He made a careful selection. He matched them up with wisdom and divine discernment. He knew which personality traits and which spiritual gifts would complement one another and contribute to the success of the mission.

We see throughout the Bible that God used spiritual partnerships or divine connections to further His purposes. These relationships not only brought success to the plan of God, but also brought comfort and strength to those in partnership together.

Where would David have been without Jonathan, who through a covenant friendship, protected David from the attempts upon his life by King Saul? Perhaps Paul would have never fulfilled his destiny, established churches, reached much of the known world, and written much of the New Testament without a divine connection with Barnabus, who brought him to Antioch to teach the believers. Pricilla and Aquilla were divinely connected, not only as husband and wife, but as co-pastors of the church which met in their home. God used them to instruct powerful leaders such as Apollos in the things of God.

Husband and wife connections are very powerful. The way that these connections work varies from one couple to another. Some may actively minister together. Others may seem to function separately. In my own case, my strongest divine connection is with my wife. Although she doesn't always travel in ministry with me, I feel united with her at all times. When I go into a meeting, almost always Susan and I have prayed together about the gathering. She will often pray things under the unction of the Holy Spirit that will be a key to the operation of my ministry in that meeting. I may be ministering among strangers, but I am not alone. We are together, though often separated physically.

We all need to discern the relationships which God has ordained for us and understand how they are to be structured, in order to fulfill the divine purpose for our lives. All too often, our prejudice, emotional reactions, natural thinking, and fleshly wisdom keep us from functioning in these vital divine connections. There are spiritual connections between husbands and wives, between ministers, between church members and their pastors which are not being fulfilled today. As a result, the Body of Christ is weaker and less able to touch the world. There are ministries that are called by God to work together. There are churches that are called to unite. There are business people who are called to divine partnership with ministries. There are friends that have been separated through disrespect, dishonor, and insensitivity. When these divine connections are broken, the work of God suffers.

Divine connections are not to be manipulated or contrived. We need to learn to flow with the Spirit in these partnerships, to connect in the way that God has ordained, and with the people to whom God has divinely connected to us.

Keep the Unity Until We Get Unity

"I therefore, the prisoner of the Lord, beseech you that ye walk worthy of the vocation wherewith ye are called, With all lowliness and meekness, with longsuffering, forbearing one another in love; Endeavouring to keep the unity of the Spirit in the bond of peace." Ephesians 4:1-3, KJV.

The book of Ephesians gives us tremendous insight into the issue of unity in the Body of Christ. The first three chapters of that book deal with our position in Christ—who we are, what we have, and what we can do as a result of our spiritual union with the Lord. Then in Ephesians 4, Paul deals with the practical outworking of our spiritual walk in the Christian life.

Before we talk about these verses, notice what Paul says in Ephesians 4:13, "Till we all come in the unity of the faith, and of the knowledge of the Son of God, unto a perfect man, unto the measure of the stature of the fulness of Christ:" Ephesians 4:13, KJV. In verse 3, he tells us to "keep the unity. . ." In verse 13, he says "till we all come into the unity." We might wonder if Paul was confused. First, he says we are to keep the unity, implying that unity is something we already possess, but need to keep. Then, he says in the future, we will come to the unity.

But in reality, he is speaking of two different types of unity—the "unity of the Spirit" and the "unity of the faith." These are two very different things.

We have the unity of the Spirit now, because "There is one body, and one Spirit, even as ye are called in one hope of your calling; One Lord, one faith, one baptism, One God and Father of all, who is above all, and through all, and in you all." Ephesians 4:4-6, KJV. You see, every born again Christian has the same Father. We are all part of the same Body, regardless of our denomination, race, or gender. We all receive from one Spirit. There is only one Lord who died for all of us, and there is only one baptism. In the mind of God, we are one.

This is why He says we are to *keep* the unity. We do not need to make unity. We are already unified. We need to earnestly guard that unity in the bond of peace. We are to have peace with one another, in spite of what differences we may have.

This is where we miss it. All too often, if someone disagrees with our theology or methodology, we are ready to declare them anathema (cursed). We are ready to break fellowship with them. But the Bible says we are to endeavor (strive earnestly) to keep the unity of the Spirit until we all come in the unity of the faith.

"Thy watchmen shall lift up the voice; with the voice together shall they sing: for they shall see eye to eye, when the LORD shall bring again Zion." Isaiah 52:8, KJV. You see, there is a day coming when we will see eye to eye. The Lord is going to bring us into the unity of the faith. But until that day, we are to endeavor to keep the the unity of the Spirit. We are to forebear (put up with) one another in love. Someone may have a different view of the Day of the Lord than me, but that does not mean he is not my brother in Christ. Someone may have a different view of spiritual gifts, but that does not mean we do not have the same Father. Someone may have a different vision on how to reach the world, but ultimately we are all going the same direction.

Don't Write One Another Off

"But why dost thou judge thy brother? or why dost thou set at nought thy brother? for we shall all stand before the judgment seat of Christ. For it is written, As I live, saith the Lord, every knee shall bow to me, and every tongue shall confess to God. So then every one of us shall give account of himself to God. Let us not therefore judge one another any more: but judge this rather, that no man put a stumblingblock or an occasion to fall in his brother's way." Romans 14:10-13, KJV.

We are often quick to "write off" our brother because of some perceived failure or doctrinal difference. We may call him a name, talk behind his back, or break fellowship. By doing this, we set a stumbling block for him and others and greatly hinder the work of God. As Christians, we are part of the family of God. We are called to love and support one another.

"And John answered him, saying, Master, we saw one casting out devils in thy name, and he followeth not us: and we forbad him, because he followeth not us. But Jesus said, Forbid him not: for there is no man which shall do a miracle in my name, that can lightly speak evil of me. For he that is not against us is on our part." Mark 9:38-40, KJV.

The disciples did not want to allow the man to use the name of Jesus, because he "followeth not us." He's not in our denomination, Jesus. He doesn't have papers with our organization. We can't allow him to minister. But Jesus made it clear that He has His servants in many different places. I've been blessed to find fellowship with believers from many different denominations, streams, and movements. We don't always agree with every jot and tittle, but where there is a love for the Lord and for souls, we can often unite and work together.

Actually, our differences can serve to strengthen us and help us to grow in new dimensions in Christ. Different perspectives on the Word are needed to help us see the whole picture. When we reject our brother's point of view, we instantly lose that perspective and he loses ours. "There is a river, the streams whereof shall make glad the city of God, the holy place of the tabernacles of the most High." Psalms 46:4, KJV. Notice that it is all the streams flowing together that make up the river of God.

I realize that there are some things that are just out-and-out heresy and need to be exposed. We need to be careful of subtle tactics of the enemy to bring error and sin into the Church. But often people are too quick to cry "false doctrine." What about your false doctrine? What about the things that you hold to be absolutely true, and yet you do not see the whole truth yet, until the Lord reveals these things. No, none of us have arrived. All of us have a ways to go, and as we are growing, we may tend to overemphasize or underemphasize certain things along the way. But if our heart is right and we are seekers of the truth, we will get where we are going, by and by. Meanwhile, let's walk in love towards our brother, so that the Father's will might be accomplished in all of us.

Our Gifts Color Our Vision

"But unto every one of us is given grace according to the measure of the gift of Christ." Ephesians 4:7, KJV.

Another source of division can be our particular gifts and callings in the Body of Christ. The way that we look at things spiritually is largely based on our gifts and callings. Just as much as we are the same—one Father, one Spirit, one Jesus, one Body— we are also different, because Jesus made us that way. We each have different gifts. A study of the gifts reveals that each member of the Body of Christ has a different perspective according to the gift that has been given to him.

For example, a person given the gift of prophecy will look at a situation differently than a person with a gift of mercy. The solution they each see for a given problem will be completely different, and because of this, they will often be at odds. But in fact, both perspectives are valid and necessary. God made each person differently, so He could use them in different ways to minister to people.

Likewise, a pastor and an evangelist may see things differently. The pastor's eyes are more on the local church and the well-being of the saints. The evangelist has his eyes more on the world and the needs of a lost and dying humanity. The evangelist needs the pastor's perspective. The pastor needs the evangelist's perspective. Together they can build the Kingdom of God. This is an example of a divine connection which is much needed in the Body of Christ today.

So, oftentimes it is our different gifting which separates us. It may also be our different religious or cultural backgrounds. It may be differences based on our gender, age, or nationality. Sometimes it is based on spiritual differences. Sometimes it is natural things. But if we can realize that it is okay to be different, and if we are willing to accept one another's differences as normal, then we can begin to build together.

The Ministers Must Flow Together

"And he gave some, apostles; and some, prophets; and some, evangelists; and some, pastors and teachers; For the perfecting of the saints, for the work of the ministry, for the edifying of the body of Christ: Till we all come in the unity of the faith, and of the knowledge of the Son of God, unto a perfect man, unto the measure of the stature of the fulness of Christ: That we henceforth be no more children, tossed to and fro, and carried about with every wind of doctrine, by the sleight of men, and cunning craftiness, whereby they lie in wait to deceive; But speaking the truth in love, may grow up into him in all things, which is the head, even Christ: From whom the whole body fitly joined together and compacted by that which every joint supplieth, according to the effectual

working in the measure of every part, maketh increase of the body unto the edifying of itself in love." Ephesians 4:11-16, KJV.

The role of the various ministers in the Body of Christ is vital to maintaining the unity of the Spirit, maturing the Body of Christ, bringing us into the unity of the faith, and reaching the world for Jesus Christ. These fivefold ministry gifts include apostles, prophets, evangelists, pastors, and teachers. Their purpose is to perfect (or mature) the saints (God's consecrated people), so that they might do the work towards building up (not tearing down) Christ's Body, the Church, until we come into the unity of faith, the knowledge of the son of God, into full maturity, becoming like Jesus. This is where we are headed, and the fivefold ministry gifts are given by God to get us there.

What an awesome responsibility we as the ministers of God have been given by the Lord to bring His Church into her destiny. No wonder James says that not many of us should be teachers, knowing that we shall receive the greater judgment. (James 3:1)

This understanding of the ministry gifts of God should also give all of us a solemn warning about how we treat the gift of God. "He that receiveth you receiveth me, and he that receiveth me receiveth him that sent me." Matthew 10:40, KJV. We must learn to respect God's vessels who He has sent. The way that we treat them is the way we are treating the

Lord. Sometimes people are quick to attack, demean, and criticize ministers of the Gospel. They may think that they are being gallant and bold by the things that they say, without realizing that they are acting completely against the will of God. As the Word of God says, "Who art thou that judgest another man's servant? to his own master he standeth or falleth. Yea, he shall be holden up: for God is able to make him stand." Romans 14:4, KJV.

The ministry gifts, too, must respect one another and work together. If the ministers (apostles, prophets, evangelists, pastors, and teachers) are the key given by the Lord Jesus Christ to bring us into the unity of the faith, then the ministers must lead the way into that unity by keeping the unity of the Spirit in the bond of peace amongst themselves, respecting one another's God-given gifts and speaking the truth in love to one another. The ministers must unite and work together to accomplish the will of God in the Church.

We must find those divine connections which God has ordained between us. We must let go of our prejudice, emotional strongholds, and hindrances to unity among the brethren. We must unite around Jesus, the head of the Church, and His great cause of reaching the world, rather than our own man-made alliances, narrow-minded cynicism, or gift-orientated biases. We must find that common denominator between us (who is Jesus) and lift Him up before the world.

If the ministers grow up, then the Body will grow up. Then God can work through all the divine connections in His Body. A supply of the Spirit will come out of every "joint" (God-ordained relationship) and the Body of Christ will be built up and reach the world for Jesus Christ.

Yes, thank God for unity. It is good and pleasant. It releases a perfumed ointment from the head which flows through the ministry gifts and touches the whole Body. It brings a refreshing which will transform the Church and touch the world. In this place, the place of unity, the Lord has ordained everlasting life. Swim in that and enjoy it, and let it touch everything around you. Let the river flow, in Jesus name.

Beckon to Your Partners

"Now when he had left speaking, he said unto Simon, Launch out into the deep, and let down your nets for a draught. And Simon answering said unto him, Master, we have toiled all the night, and have taken nothing: nevertheless at thy word I will let down the net. And when they had this done, they inclosed a great multitude of fishes: and their net brake. And they beckoned unto their partners, which were in the other ship, that they should come and help them. And they came, and filled both the ships, so that they began to sink." Luke 5:4-7, KJV.

God is calling forth an army of people united in the great purpose of the hour, to bring in the

133

harvest. One person cannot bring in a great harvest alone. Like the slogan of a church I visited in Canada stated, "Teamwork makes the dream work."

Peter and the disciples' supernatural fishing expedition with Jesus illustrates this truth. Fishing for souls without Jesus can be empty, futile, and fruitless. We need His power and direction to fill the nets, to bring in the harvest. Jesus told Simon Peter, "Let down your nets for a draught." In other words, "You're going to get a great catch. Just let down your nets and I will fill them."

Peter said, "Lord we've been fishing all night and haven't caught a thing. It certainly isn't going to do any good to let them down again. But because You said it, I will let down the net." (paraphrase) Notice Jesus said "nets" but Peter said "net." Jesus always has a bigger vision than we do. And His vision requires "all hands on deck," rather than a one-man show. They were to let down the nets, but all the faith Peter could muster was to let down one net.

As he dropped the net into the water, he felt the weight of the sinkers on the net, pulling. The resistance began to increase more and more, and one by one the fisherman on Peter's boat grasped the net with all their might. The force of the weight became so great it began to tear apart the net. The fabric of their harvesting machine was being ripped apart. Then, they called for their partners in another ship.

This is the great need in the Body of Christ—partners. Partners are needed to bring in a great catch—prayer partners, financial partners, churches partnering, ministries partnering. To bring in the great harvest, we must work together.

It's time for change in the Body of Christ. It's time for us to unite and to be about the Father's business. When we see the Lord's vision for glory in the Church, our divisions and struggles will melt away.

It's only by working together that we will see the great harvest. True unity can only be achieved by focusing on the same things—particularly one Father, one Savior, and one cause. When we focus on these things, other things will take their proper place. "Look to the fields," Jesus said, "the fields are white unto harvest." The harvest is of primary importance, and I'm willing to set aside my pet doctrines and spiritual idiosyncrasies in order to see the harvest come in.

Organizing for Success

This unity, or working together, must take a practical form. Within the local church, it means reorganizing according to the priority of the harvest. We must see the Great Commission as the thing of greatest importance in the life of the church and prioritize our finances, our labors and our prayers to line up with that priority. Everyone must be focused on bringing in the harvest. Sunday school teachers, pastors, ushers, greeters, deacons, elders, children, teens, worship leaders, marriage ministries, social coordinators, and janitors must all see their role in bringing in the harvest. Just like my neighbor at harvest time, everyone has a part to play in getting that grain in the bins, even those who bring sandwiches to the fields for the workers. Everyone's part is essential to the goal.

Once I was listening to the radio on the way home from a ministry trip here in Minnesota. I was listening to WCCO out of Minneapolis. The particular program was the Minnesota Twins Magazine.

The guest on the program was Jim Rantz, the director of the Twins minor league operation. Now, Minnesotans are pretty proud of their baseball team. After all, Minneapolis-St. Paul is a small market, and the Twins are not well funded, compared to many major league teams, and yet the Twins seem to come out near the top of their division most years and even won the World Series in 1991.

As I listened to Rantz that day, I began to understand why. You see, the Twins have become a consistent contender year after year, not by luring talent away from other teams with big salaries, but by raising exceptional players from their farm clubs. They develop the talent from beneath and raise them up. Often, they lose these players through free agency when they become successful, but by then they have someone else raised up to take their place. The Minnesota Twins are organized for success.

Rantz began to describe the teams in the farm system. He talked about the various players—their batting averages, their earned run averages, their skill levels, their mental agility, their potential. He talked about how they might fit into the Twins future plans and how the team would continue to be developed in the months and years to come. I was amazed at the command and the scope of information on the tip of Rantz's tongue, but what struck me more than anything was the seriousness and the intensity of this tremendous effort to raise up players for one purpose—to win a game played between 18 players on a patch of grass with a small round hard ball and a piece of wood.

My thought was, "If these people have become this organized and focused in order to achieve the goal of sporting success, what are we in the Church doing?" Our effort is often haphazard. We often do not take seriously the business of winning souls. We put more effort into wedding programs and carpet colors than in the real business of the Church. We need to refocus, reprioritize, reorganize, refinance, and reignite our efforts. We need to get serious about training people and releasing them to reach the lost. In many churches, there is no clear plan to reach the lost or to make disciples. In some churches, the Gospel message is seldom preached. There may be great teachings about how to live successfully or how to have a positive outlook on life, but no one stands up and tells the people on a regular basis, "You must be born again!"

The people in our churches are not hearing the message that Christ died for our sins according the Scriptures, He was buried, and He rose again. Church members seldom hear about the awful judgment for those who do not receive Christ and the clear biblical way God has given for us to escape the wrath of God. We must get back to preaching the Gospel and calling people to repentance. And we must train Christians to share their faith with others. This is the real business of the Church of Jesus Christ.

Dear Father, I thank You for the Body of Christ. I thank You that I can be a part of reaching the world, along with my brothers and sisters in Christ all around the world. Help us to love one another and work together effectively for Your great cause. Help us to put our focus on the things that are most important to Your heart and to get organized, so that the world may know that You have sent Jesus to die for their sins, in Jesus' name. Amen.

Chapter 12

What's Hindering You?

"Now I would not have you ignorant, brethren, that oftentimes I purposed to come unto you, (but was let hitherto,) that I might have some fruit among you also, even as among other Gentiles. I am debtor both to the Greeks, and to the Barbarians; both to the wise, and to the unwise. So, as much as in me is, I am ready to preach the gospel to you that are at Rome also. For I am not ashamed of the gospel of Christ: for it is the power of God unto salvation to every one that believeth; to the Jew first, and also to the Greek." Romans 1:13-16, KJV.

The Apostle Paul was someone who lived his life for the cause of Christ. This passage in Romans reveals both his struggle and his commitment to fulfill his destiny in Christ. I want you to notice several statements which will point you toward success in finishing your course in Jesus Christ:

"I was hindered." Paul had purposed in his heart to preach the Gospel at Rome, but he was hindered from doing so. (The word translated "let" in the King James Version means hindered.) In fact, other Christians even discouraged him from going there. Many times we start out to do something for the Lord, but when the going gets rough, we give up on the dream. Because all the pieces of the puzzle do not immediately come together, we think, "This must not be God." But the first rule of success is determination. We must follow through and fulfill our call.

"I am a debtor." Paul saw his call to reach the world with the Gospel as an obligation, rather than an option. He was in debt, not to Mastercard and Visa and this world system, but to God, to fulfill the Lord's mission to take the Gospel to the world. The cares of the world so often quench the zeal of God in believers, because somewhere in their mind they have determined that something else is more important than helping hurting people and bringing the Gospel to a lost and dying world.

"I am ready." The Scripture talks about having a "ready mind" or an attitude of preparedness. Are you ready today to do God's will? Preparedness is not only about education and training, but also a deep inward commitment to the purposes of God. This is an inward surrender to the will of the Father for your life. Living for today will not prepare us to be world changers for Christ tomorrow. We must sell out to the cause and be prepared for deployment as the Commander-in-Chief directs us.

"I am not ashamed." Paul was beaten, stoned, mocked, and criticized for the Gospel, but he did not let man's opinion stop him from fulfilling his mission. Even though others did not always recognize it, he knew that the Gospel is the power of God unto salvation for everyone that believes— Jew, Greek, male, female—everyone. God so loved the world that He gave His Son. The questions that we must face as believers are "Will we walk in the love of God toward a lost and dying world? And are we willing to sacrifice that others might find Christ?"

Success in the Christian ministry is not defined by the size of your budget or the number of people in your church or how many you have on your mailing list. Success is becoming Christlike. The ultimate goal of the Christian life is be like Jesus, to walk in the love of God, and to give yourself that others may find Him. Maybe you've been hindered in reaching that goal up until now, but get ready. God has a plan and a purpose for you. If you are willing to move with Him in this hour, if you are sold out, God can use you!

Is There Not a Cause?

When David saw a need in his generation, he rose up to do something about it. The great Philistine giant, Goliath, had challenged God's people and caused them to tremble. But the little shepherd boy, David, rose up against his enemy saying, "who is this uncircumcised Philistine, that he should defy the armies of the living God." (1 Sam. 17:26)

David saw the need and he responded to it with boldness. He did not sit idly by and wait for someone else to deal with the problem. He knew that with the help of God he could defeat the enemy and bring victory to the people of God.

His brother Eliab, however, questioned his motives and belittled his teenage brother. "Eliab's anger was kindled against David, and he said, Why camest thou down hither? and with whom hast thou left those few sheep in the wilderness? I know thy pride, and the naughtiness of thine heart; for thou art come down that thou mightest see the battle." (1 Samuel 17:28, KJV).

Even today, if you stand up for a cause greater than yourself, if you make a bold pronouncement against the enemy, some will belittle you and accuse you of pride. If so, let your answer be like that of the shepherd boy, David, who replied: "What have I now done? Is there not a cause?" (1 Samuel 17:29, KJV).

Don't let your focus be on the nay sayers and the critics, nor on the problems and difficulties along the way. Focus on the Lord Himself and His great cause, the Great Commission. Speak words of boldness and words of faith, like David spoke to Saul, "Thy servant slew both the lion and the bear: and this uncircumcised Philistine shall be as one of them, seeing he hath defied the armies of the living God." (1 Samuel 17:36, KJV)

Just take a minute to shout now and let the devil know that you are not about to buy the lie, but you are serving the Almighty God of the universe and you will succeed in your mission. Praising God stills the voice of the devil and will exalt the Lord over every situation. Start praising Him right now.

Go ahead. Just have a good time of it. Praise God, forevermore!

So, evangelist, witness, servant of Christ, what are you going to do? What's your plan? Where's God's compass pointing? Don't just sit there. Do something! Dust off your armor. Pull down the will of the Father in prayer. Pop a breath mint and go get 'em! I encourage you, take the limits off of God. Believe for greater things. Rise up. Arise in the glory of the Lord, for this is your hour. This is the hour of greater glory and greater works. You can touch the world!

Thank You Father, for the great privilege of representing You on this earth. I will arise and take Your Gospel to the world. I will not fear, for You are with me. Thank You Father for Jesus Christ and Your great plan of redemption. May my life give You glory and honor. I believe that by Your grace I can touch the world, in Jesus' name. Amen.

Contact us!

Has this book touched your life? It's our desire to bless you, encourage you, and help you to fulfill your destiny in this life and in the life to come. Write to us and tell us about what God is doing in your life. We'd love to pray with you and keep in touch with you through our free monthly newsletter. Check out our website. We have resources available both online and by mail to help and encourage you in your journey of faith. May God bless you abundantly, in Jesus' name.

Tom and Susan Shanklin
PO Box 4144
Mankato, MN 56002
Website: www.tomshanklin.org
Email: tom@shanklinministries.org

Tom and Susan Shanklin

Tom Shanklin and his wife Susan are both part of the baby-boomer generation that sprung up in America after the end of the Second World War. Rejecting what they saw as the hypocrisy of mainstream society, they embraced the hippie lifestyle in the '70s and became involved in a life of drug use and experimenting with various forms of religion and spirituality.

In 1977, they both had dramatic spiritual encounters and their lives were radically transformed by the living Christ. Jesus became real to them and He became the Lord of their lives. Their ministry was birthed out of that transformation along with a desire to see others come to Christ. They served as pastors in various local churches in Minnesota and North Dakota for 22 years, along with traveling nationally and internationally and publishing the Gospel in various forms, including a Christian newspaper called the Heartland News.

The focus of their ministry since 2005 has been evangelism, cross-cultural missions, and living the Christian life in practical ways with their family and in their community. Tom and Susan have three grown children and three grandchildren who give them great joy.

Tom Shanklin is motivated by a desire to see people reunited with God, healed (spiritually, emotionally, and physically), and filled with a sense of their divine purpose in life. He preaches in a simple and practical way that people of all ages, nations, and denominations can receive. Tom ministers within the United States as well as internationally encouraging people in their walk with God and exalting the message of the cross of Jesus Christ as the answer to their deepest need.

Susan Shanklin brings a powerful and unique approach to the Gospel of Jesus Christ. Her straightforward method brings conviction and empowerment into people's lives by applying the Scriptures to real life situations. She is bold and compassionate in her presentation and has a special ability to make people laugh and to look at things in a fresh new way, both through her preaching and through her unique writing style. Susan is also an accomplished stained glass artist and enjoys the homesteading lifestyle on the couple's farm site in southern Minnesota.

Tom Shanklin Ministries

"Go ye into all the world, and preach the gospel to every creature." Mark 16:15, KJV.

Tom Shanklin Ministries is an interdenominational, international ministry dedicated to taking the whole Gospel to the whole world. Through our partnership with churches, ministries, and individuals, we are bringing a message of *Good News for Everyone.*

The foundation of this ministry is Jesus Christ, and the work that He accomplished when He was sent to the earth by God our Father, died on the cross of Calvary for our sins, and rose again from the dead to give us victory over sin, death, and the devil. The Holy Spirit is anointing Christian believers all around the world to bring this message of spiritual, emotional, physical, and relational healing to a lost, hurting, and needy world. As we unite, we see multitudes finding the peace, rest, and healing that comes from knowing Jesus Christ as Lord and Savior.

Tom Shanklin Ministries is not limited to working with one denomination, group, stream, or local church, but we are called by God to unite with Christ's entire body to bring in the harvest in these last days. We share in the common goal of reaching the world with the Good News of Jesus Christ.

To accomplish our goal, we:

- Pray for the nations.
- Preach the Good News.
- Provide encouragement, training, and leadership.
- Publish the Gospel through every available medium.
- Promote life-giving ministries around the world.

We invite you to join hands with us, as the Holy Spirit leads you, to see a great harvest of souls in the earth, that Jesus may be lifted up and our heavenly Father may be glorified. For scheduling or more information, contact:

Tom Shanklin
M I N I S T R I E S

PO Box 4144 Mankato, MN 56002 USA
Website: www.tomshanklin.org
Email: tom@shanklinministries.org

Books and CDs by Tom Shanklin

Filling the Void

A Journey from Darkness to Light

Tom Shanklin and his wife Susan embraced the hippie lifestyle in the '70s and became involved in a life of drug use and experimenting with various forms of religion and spirituality. In 1977, they both had dramatic spiritual encounters and their lives were radically transformed by the living Christ. Jesus became real to them and He became the Lord of their lives. *Filling the Void* is the story of that transformation and a message for everyone who senses an emptiness inside and is longing for a powerful and meaningful change in their lives.

The Healing CD

Healing Scriptures and Prayers

Originally released as *The Healing Tape,* this valuable tool has helped many to find divine healing through God's Word. It's not a sermon, but rather a collection of scriptures, confessions, and prayers designed to help the sick regain sound health in their spirit, soul, and body. With a voice of compassion and strength, Tom leads the listeners on a journey of healing in the Word of God. As you listen to these powerful scriptures and prayers, your faith will come alive for healing in every area of your life.

You Can Touch the World

A How-to Manual for Reaching the World for Christ

You Can Touch the World will unveil the awesome potential of your life and inspire you to take the challenge to touch your world with the love of God. With Christ's direction and plan in your life, you can make a difference. You can have the power to bring change, to impart life that only comes from the heart of the Father. When you act on God's plan, you are acting out of love, out of concern, out of compassion. You are putting the throbbing heartbeat of the Father into action. His heart beats for people—lost, hurting sighing, dying humanity—people who are far away from Him. You are the key to bringing them home. You are the extension of the heart of the Father.

You Can Touch the World is a great tool for:

- Local Churches
- Home Groups
- Evangelism Classes
- Outeach Teams
- Bible Studies

You can order these materials by visiting our website at www.tomshanklin.org

Made in the USA
Charleston, SC
29 August 2011